Susan Burrows Swan

PLATE 1

PLAIN & FANCY

PLATE 2

# PLAIN

## American Women and

### Susan Burrows Swan

A Rutledge Book

# & FANCY

## Their Needlework, 1700–1850

Special Photography by George J. Fistrovich

Holt, Rinehart and Winston/New York

PLATE 3

*Editorial Director:* Fred R. Sammis
*Creative Director:* John T. Sammis
*Editor in Chief:* Jeanne McClow
*Art Director:* Allan Mogel
*Production Director:* Julianne J. Griffin
*Editor:* Jeremy Friedlander
*Associate Editor:* Lee Hoeting
*Associate Art Director:* David Namias
*Production Manager:* Lori Stein
*Editorial Assistants:* Susan Lurie, Candida Pilla

Library of Congress Cataloging in Publication Data
Swan, Susan Burrows.
   Plain and fancy.
   "A Rutledge book."
   Bibliography: p. 235
   Includes index.
   1.   Needlework—United States—History   I.   Title.
TT715.S9      301.41'2      77-1627
ISBN 0-03-015121-X

First Edition
Printed in Italy by Mondadori, Verona
10 9 8 7 6 5 4 3 2 1

*Glossary illustrations by Carol Hines*

*All items illustrated are owned by
the Henry Francis du Pont Winterthur Museum
unless otherwise specified.*

*Abbreviations Used in the Captions:*
H = height   W = width   cm = centimeters
DMMC, WM = Joseph Downs Manuscript and Microfilm Collection,
           Henry Francis du Pont Winterthur Museum Libraries

**Plate 1** *An early nineteenth-century woman's hollow-cut silhouette stamped
MUSEUM, from the museum that Charles Willson Peale operated in
Independence Hall, Philadelphia. Author's collection.*

**Plate 2** *One of the most artistically drawn and executed Boston "fishing lady"
pictures known. Unfortunately, it is unsigned. The tent-stitched canvas work is
done with crewel and silk with accents of metallic yarns. Each of the three
groups of figures recur on other Boston-type pictures, alone or in combination.
For a cluster of the most appealing dogs in needlework, see the detail of this
picture, Figure 25. 1745–55; H. 21" (53.34 cm); W. 42" (106.68 cm).*

**Plate 3** *A 1737 sampler in the earlier, long and narrow style by ten-year-old
Jane Simons. It is uncommon to find an eighteenth-century sampler worked in
crewel yarns, as this one is. Someone experimented with a few drawn work
stitches in linen thread near one of the tulips. Originally, a sampler like this
would not have been framed but kept rolled up and brought out when needed for
reference. History of ownership in Oyster Bay, Long Island; H. 20 15/16"
(53.18 cm); W. 8 5/16" (21.20 cm).*

# Contents

# Preface

This book began years ago when I realized that needlework offered early American women their primary outlet for creative expression. Indeed, except for needlework, almost no tangible products made by the women of centuries past remain. It occurred to me that surviving needlework projects represent one of our few remaining links with one half of our ancestors.

My study started with the objects. At the Henry Francis du Pont Winterthur Museum alone, there are more than six hundred pieces of American needlework. By arranging these and other pieces according to their techniques and dates, and by allowing for variations in individual abilities, I began to see a pattern in the development of the needle crafts in America. The finest work was done before 1785. Between 1785 and 1825, the work was proficient but not as fine as that done earlier. And from 1825 to 1875, a marked deterioration in needlework skills became apparent.

In an effort to understand these trends, I turned to primary sources. Eighteenth- and nineteenth-century newspapers contain valuable data from hundreds of advertisements by schools, listing the kinds of training they offered young women. By charting these advertisements according to the needlework forms and stitches, academic subjects, and other accomplishments they referred to, and by correlating this information with locations and dates, I gained a more precise idea of what needlework was being done where during the different periods. The Glossary contains much of this data.

Women's magazines of the eighteenth century offered philosophy by and about women that helps to explain some of the changes in the needlework of the past. In particular, the more widely read, less expensive nineteenth-century magazines reveal a dramatic connection between women's lives and their needlework, if only in that these periodicals included specific needlework instructions virtually side by side with their columns of advice to women. Inventories and wills hold clues as to the importance of possessions. Finally, private thoughts recorded in diaries, journals, letters, and recollections, as well as public pronouncements by ministers, editors, and "manner" books, reveal the emotional state and ideas of the day

I realized that in these sources I had at best a representative sample of what only a small group of women were thinking. To cite the most obvious limitations of this material: The women who were committing their personal feelings to diaries or recording their day's activities in journals were a small portion of the minority of women literate enough to keep such records. Women who wrote for publication—a daring act even in the more enlightened days of early American life—represented an even more select few. And the role models urged upon women of the past, like role models today, represented no one at all; they were models, not real people.

Fortunately, the women who did decorative, or "fancy," needlework corresponded fairly closely to the women who read or produced this literature. These women, whom I have sometimes referred to here as "of the better sort," were usually but not always wealthy, relatively well educated, and, most important, socially successful, or "genteel," to use a term that accomplished ladies favored to describe themselves. Moreover, particularly before 1800, the surviving fancy needlework tends to have been made in the same towns and cities from which we also have newspaper records. If one cannot gain a completely accurate picture of these women from the newspapers and magazines they read and from the diaries and journals a few of them left, one can make a more educated guess about them than about the housewives, far more numerous, who left behind no written records. As only "plain" needleworkers, common housewives have a lesser part in this story.

This book has been titled Plain and Fancy because that common sewing term summarizes the lives of women as well as their needlework. But unlike the lives of early American women, there is more fancy than plain here. Fancy is of course more fun, not only for the women who did it, but for people today, such as myself, who enjoy needlework both for how it strikes us aesthetically and for what it tells us about the women who created it.

In organizing this book, I chose to keep the plain and the fancy—both women and their needlework—as distinctly separate as possible. Although the different segments of early American society shared many practices, customs, and beliefs, there were distinct divisions among them. For example, only the "middling" and "better sorts" of women could afford to do fancy needlework. Thus, the first chapter in the book, "Plain Sewing, Plain Housewives," covers a common denominator of women's lives and their sewing, and the rest of the book limits itself to the women who did fancy sewing. Chapter 2 traces the evolution in the education of young ladies, because the trends in education provide an excellent insight into the changes in needlework styles and the changing roles of women. Then the last three chapters treat the three basic eras of fancy needlework, as mentioned above—1720-1785, 1785-1825, and 1825-1875.

I have divided the different needlework forms into these eras, mindful of the fact that there would inevitably be overlap. For example, American women were quilting long before the nineteenth century, but I chose to examine quilting in the last chapter, for reasons that should become clear there. A century and a half of American women and their needlework is a multifaceted subject, defying quick and easy structural breakdown. In any attempt such as this to determine not only how people lived but what they thought and how they expressed their thoughts through their art, the most delicate matter of all is to dramatize change without overstating it. If I have established needlework in a historical context that is both accurate and clear, then I have succeeded.

❖ ❖ ❖ ❖ ❖

The research for this project has often been most absorbing to me, and the transformation of the results into a book has been a great challenge. I have been exceptionally fortunate in encountering many people of very generous natures, both during the research and in the writing of the book. Colleagues at the Henry Francis du Pont Winterthur Museum to whom I am especially grateful are: Nancy Goyne Evans, Registrar, who not only shared her own research with me but generously aided me in numerous thoughtful ways; Arlene Palmer, Assistant Curator; Karol Schmeigel, Assistant Registrar, Deborah Waters, Librarian, Decorative Arts Photographic Collection; Benno Forman, Research Fellow and Teaching Associate; E. McSherry Fowble, Associate Curator; Kathleen MacIntire, Senior

Guide; Frank Sommers, Head, Libraries Division; Eleanor Thompson, Associate Librarian; Elizabeth Hill, former Librarian, Manuscript and Microfilm Collection; Beatrice Taylor, Librarian, Manuscript and Microfilm Collection; and Katherine McKenney, Librarian, Photography and Slide Collection.

Another joy of being associated with the Winterthur Museum has been the experience of teaching in the Decorative Arts Program of the University of Delaware and learning from its Fellows. The knowledge, curiosity, and generosity of David Schuyler have been enormously encouraging. Page Talbot Gould, Robert Trent, David Kiehl, and June Sprigg also all shared their ideas and research materials.

I am indebted to a number of kind and helpful friends, collectors, and scholars: Davida and Alvin Deutsch, Sandra Downie, George J. Fistrovich, Jean and Joseph McFalls, Carol and Robert Baker, Betty Ring, Karen Hill, Alberta Brandt, Darlene Scott, Polly Stocker, David Santuary Howard, Ruth and Theodore Kapnek, and Frederick Weiser.

The Chester County Historical Society allowed me to include some of its superb collection in the illustrations. A trustee of the Winterthur Museum, R. Philip Hanes, Jr., permitted me to publish the Gilbert Stuart portrait of the young ladies doing tambour work included here.

George J. Fistrovich conceived the innovative idea of photographing the needlework in settings that suggest their original ones. I appreciate his originality, artistry, and cooperation. Thanks, too, to Catherine Hutchins of Winterthur's Publications Office for graciously sharing her historical knowledge and to Carol Hines, who did the fine drawings for the glossary. To the people at Rutledge Books who contributed their very special talents, I express my deep gratitude: Jeanne McClow, Editor in Chief; Allan Mogel, Art Director; Lee Hoeting, Associate Editor; David Namias, Associate Art Director; and particularly Jeremy Friedlander, Editor, whose skill and creativity made this book possible.

Most of all, I am indebted to my husband and sons, who gave their help, support, and love.

Susan Burrows Swan

FIGURE

# Introduction

**Figure 1** *A moralistic print for women, defining the boundaries they should observe in their lives. Entitled "Keep Within Compass"; unsigned sepia engraving; United States or England; 1785–1800.*

Through the years in the more affluent cultures, men have traditionally relegated women to playing the decorative, seemingly subservient roles, and women have allowed this. Perhaps it made most women feel pampered, protected, freed from the pressures of coping. Except for some wonderful, rare rebels, whose words we shall quote in this book, it took until the mid-twentieth century for American women to demand and expect a more fully egalitarian society.

Nevertheless, some of our female ancestors were incredible women. From early on they were brave and able, often working beside their men, sharing responsibility, building this country with their own hands. They bore children, buried children and husbands, and survived. On the frontier, they helped to clear the forests, work the fields, chop wood, build fences, defend their homes and families. They tended children, grew vegetable gardens, made candles and soap, cooked, cared for livestock, and fished. A few exceptional women were painters, poets, and writers. A few even fought in war, marching with the armies and bearing arms. There were also some skilled women—blacksmiths, printers, engravers, and silversmiths. They ran businesses, engaged in commerce, administered property.

Beyond and above all the things they did, they sewed. And they taught their daughters to sew. Their needlework took two forms—"plain" and "fancy." Plain sewing included the essential forms of household needlework—the cutting out and stitching of underwear, ordinary clothing, sheets, towels, bedcoverings. This work required simple stitches, among them the back, whip, cross, and running stitches. Knitting and the marking of household linen fit into this category. All women had to do plain sewing, or make provisions to get it done.

Fancy needlework encompassed all the nonutilitarian forms. Since purely decorative work by its very nature was superfluous, only women in comfortable financial circumstances enjoyed the leisure time that enabled them to indulge in it. Most surviving needlework artifacts are fancywork. This is not surprising, for they were cherished mementoes, passed down through generations, whereas plain work was consumed—used and reused, cut down and remodeled, until only the scraps remained to be finally used in quilts.

This book's purpose is to show the integral part needlework played in the lives of these women, particularly how it allowed them to express themselves in an almost completely male-dominated society. For needlework, in addition to being the most important contribution made by early American women to the decorative arts, was also their most acceptable outlet for creative expression and, indeed, in many instances the only concrete evidence of their endeavors. Needlework tells us a good deal about what it was like to be a woman in early America.

Throughout this period of history, almost no women, not even those of the upper classes, could escape the basic requirements of their sex. These included marrying, bearing and rearing one's children, and taking care of a load of household chores, of which plain sewing was only one. This, the basic role of the common housewife, was the basic role of all women from 1700 to 1850. Even the stylish lady for the most part remained in essence a housewife and mother.

It was a life of unrelenting hardship for many women. For them, plain sewing occupied only a small part of the day, and it often came as a relief from the arduous drudgery that was their normal lot. To our eyes plain sewing seems an uninspiring aspect of her life, yet it had to be done, and a woman got it done without question or complaint, just as she got married, had babies, and ran the household. For a woman, plain sewing was an inescapable part of an inescapable life-style.

For the wives or daughters of prosperous men, plain sewing had added significance: It was the essential first step in learning fancy needlework, a stylish lady's most important accomplishment. For the most part, young ladies went to school to cultivate the traits that would attract a husband. Fancy needlework was invariably a part of their education, often the only part. More scholarly training came as an extra, since a cultivated intellect usually did not help a female either to attract a man or to serve him as his wife. Through the ups and downs in female education over this one-hundred-fifty-year period, one overriding theme remained—the subordination of a woman's mind to her duties as wife and mother. Even so enlightened an observer as Dr. Benjamin Rush, physician, statesman, and social commentator, who called for women to be "governed by reason," did not challenge the basic assumption that they should be obedient housewives and dutiful mothers.[1]

Society consistently failed to appreciate the intellectual capabilities of its women. Yet in cultivating other qualities in them, it sometimes genuinely encouraged their self-expression and fulfillment. In the eighteenth century before the Revolution, craftsmanship flourished in the colonies, and the women who did fancy needlework during this period must be considered on a par with the other fine craftsmen of the day.

These women, however, were still housewives, albeit well-to-do ones, who almost literally did their fancywork while they ran their households. Legally they were wards of their husbands; socially they were adornments to them. Practically, however, they were nearly their equals. These women stayed home because they had to—to oversee the smooth functioning of their households—but many of them also left the home because they had to—to assist their husbands in business and even to take over the businesses as widows. These were sober, resourceful, meticulous workers, in their fancy needlework and in their lives.

After the Revolution, the leisure class that had begun to develop in the colonies as early as the first half of the eighteenth century emerged in full flower. The women who belonged to it had tasted the eighteenth-century equivalent of the good life, and they wanted to keep it, even as they rebelled against many of the more confining strictures on women. These women no longer had the time or inclination for the precise, unassuming craftsmanship that had marked needlework done earlier in the century. In short, this was a time of rising expectations.

A few enlightened thinkers were advancing radically new suggestions for improving women's opportunities, but there was little change in women's substantive status. The women of this age were likely to have been more sophisticated and better educated than their predecessors, but in general they too remained ornaments to their husbands. If anything, the idea of woman-as-adornment grew stronger. In the nineteenth century, women became ensconced in the home even more securely than before and lost many of the common, if unspoken, freedoms they had enjoyed earlier, in a less-structured society. The Victorian Age had descended.

In this, the final period discussed in this book, the exquisite fancy sewing of the eighteenth century all but disappeared, and in its place the uninspired copy stitching called "Berlin work" became fashionable. As Victorian society and industrialism foreclosed any other options, most well-off women found themselves assigned to the home, rededicated to serving their families. They continued to work with their sewing needles, almost as industriously as before, but the era of fine needlework had passed.

❖ ❖ ❖ ❖ ❖

In 1815, an iconoclastic seventeen-year-old, Mehetable May Dawes of Massachusetts, reflected, "All men feel so grand and boast so much . . .

about being lords of the world below. . . . we are very willing men should *think* they govern since they are happier for so thinking while to ourselves we laugh at the deception."[2] The appearance of subservience was well maintained by fancy needlework. It allowed women to posture prettily and to create lovely articles. It was feminine and delicate and ornamental, and harked back to the docile scene of Penelope patiently weaving as she waited for the return of Ulysses.

Consider, for example, the engraving "Keep Within Compass," published in the third quarter of the eighteenth century (Figure 1). A well-dressed lady strolls serenely in a garden, tatting while she walks, for even at leisure she is industrious, her hands never idle. The compass is a symbol that openly acknowledges the rigid confines of her status, for only by obeying the rules could she become "A Virtuous Woman [who] is a Crown to her Husband." She is admonished to "Keep Within Compass And You Shall Be Sure to Avoid Many Troubles Which Others Endure."

To drive home the message, the engraver has depicted in the corner vignettes some of the pitfalls to which a woman of the times might fall prey. For example, she might take to drink (upper right) and neglect her child as she becomes addicted to card playing and gambling (upper left). This in turn might lead her to prostitution. In the third vignette (lower right) she is shown soliciting a man, when a night watchman intervenes. And finally, the ultimate degradation—a hopeless life in prison (lower left).

Needlework, then, was well within the most restrictive compass of a woman's possibilities—a sort of garnish to it. Indeed for many generations, handwork and fancy sewing epitomized the ideal woman.

But there is more to the story. For if fancy needlework was a symbol of a woman's way of life, and it was, that way of life was not always as rigidly confining as the puritanical exhortation "Keep Within Compass" makes it appear. In her needlework a woman was expressive and often creative. At these moments she gave us a revealing insight into her character and her times. If nothing else, these achievements help us to see some real and remarkable people beneath the cloak of domesticity and subservience, which for the most part has shrouded our perceptions of these women.

# 1 Plain Sewing, Plain Housewives

Every early American girl learned plain needlework, usually starting as soon as she could manipulate a needle. A common girl certainly had to know how to sew because as a housewife she would have to make and mend all the cloth products her family needed—not only clothing but bed linens and towels, too. A wealthy girl needed to know how to sew, too, because she would have to deal with more clothing, bed linens, and towels—plus curtains and table linens—and she was not likely to be able to pay someone else to do all the plain sewing her household required. She could delegate much of the work to servants or slaves, but in that case she needed to know enough to direct them, and she might even have to teach them. Besides, without knowing the simple and basic techniques of plain sewing, she could not begin to learn fancy needlework (Figure 2).

Plain sewing was so basic to any girl's training that a girl who couldn't sew was considered odd, certainly not ready for marriage. And marriage was not merely a goal in life for a girl; it was her mission. She heard enough derogatory remarks about spinsters (also known as "thorn-backs," "stale virgins," "antick virgins," "stale maids," and "old maids") and witnessed enough contemptuous treatment of them to understand very early that if she were to fail to marry, she would bring not only unhappiness but a measure of social disgrace on herself and her family. To win a husband and to serve him well, she had to know how to sew.

Moreover, plain sewing provided a woman who had little or no help in her household with an opportunity to sit down for a while and let her mind wander, all the while secure in the knowledge that she was doing something productive, keeping her hands busy. This was an important consideration, for to be idle was thought to be sinful. As the Reverend Isaac Watts, author of *Divine Songs for Children*, a popular source of sampler verses, wrote, "Satan finds some mischief still for idle hands to do."

Plain sewing was a task that lent itself to socializing, too. A woman could bring it with her when she went out visiting, or she could pick it up while socializing at home. Because it required no great attention, she could join in the conversation or listen while someone else read aloud.

In itself, plain sewing could be either arduous and repetitive or relaxing and almost therapeutic, probably depending on the particular task

**Figure 2** *Four examples of well-marked household linens worked entirely in cross-stitch; United States; 1800–25.*

18

and the needlewoman's mood. The products of the work—fresh, new sheets, pillowcases, linen towels, and chemises—could provide a woman with a great deal of satisfaction with her skill and her contribution to the household. For the woman who made her own outer clothing, the completion of a new or even a remade gown must have been a specially pleasurable event.

Before colonial women could do plain sewing, however, there had to be fabric to work with. It is difficult for us in this industrial age to appreciate fully the value that was assigned to most textiles during the seventeenth and eighteenth centuries. They were, in fact, considered so important that inventories of household possessions listed them immediately after land holdings, money, and silver. Since repairing and reusing clothing was far less costly and time-consuming than making it new, a garment was mended and remodeled over and over again until the fabric became so badly worn that it was cut down and remade into a garment for a younger, smaller member of the family. And when the smallest child had finally worn through it, it could be cut up and pieced together to make a bed quilt. Consequently, few examples of plain clothing survive as such today. The more elaborate garments we have from this time are nearly all remodeled versions of the originals.

Several factors accounted for the high value of textiles. For one thing, during colonial days, cotton was not the basic textile that it is today. Before the Revolution, most of the cotton that came to the colonies was grown in India and then shipped to England for processing, either as fiber or as cloth. Although cotton mills began operating in New England, New York, and New Jersey in the late 1780s, it was not until well into the nineteenth century, with the successful domestic cultivation of the more widely grown and more easily carded short-staple cotton, that cotton yarn and fabrics became inexpensive and hence popular in the United States.

Silk fabrics were even rarer during the colonial period. Although a family might grow its own mulberry trees and cultivate silkworms, the rest of the silk-making process required too much labor to support profitable large-scale commercial production. The process called for a silk reeler, who would unwind the fibers and twist them into thread. Then a weaver would turn the threads into fabric by means of special hand looms. One such craftsman, fringe-and-lace-maker James Butland, advertised in the August 15, 1774, issue of the *Pennsylvania Packet* that "any person having silk of their own may have it manufactured into . . . silk stockings, sewing silk, ribbons &c." After the Revolutionary War, American ships began regular voyages to China and brought back silk at steadily decreasing—though still not low—prices. By about 1830, the competition of foreign silk put the continually faltering American silk makers out of business.

Because both cotton and silk were scarce during the colonial period, most clothing and household items of fabric were made from English and European linen or wool. Small amounts of these fabrics, generally lower grades, were domestically produced. Many people could afford to buy such cloth, and newspaper listings of fabrics for sale (not only wool and linen, but also cotton and silk) made up perhaps the greatest single category of newspaper advertisements. Other people, however, particularly those living in rural areas, had to rely on home-produced yarn, which meant starting from scratch by raising flax for linen or sheep for wool.

The elementary steps involved in making fabrics were tedious, time-consuming, and, in the case of home production, mostly the province of women. Spinning was one such woman's activity, often assigned to an unmarried sister or daughter living with the family or, in wealthier circles, to a servant or slave. The task was more dreary than onerous, which suited the period's stereotype of single women; because these women were often the ones who did spinning, the derogatory connotation of the word *spinster* evolved.

The type of spinning wheel that the spinster used depended on the type of fiber she was working with. The wheel for wool was large and was turned by hand. Sometimes called a walking wheel, it required the woman to back away from the wheel while she spun the yarn and then move forward toward the wheel to wrap it onto the spindle. Obviously, producing yarn on a walking wheel could be wearisome. The wheel for flax was smaller and was operated by a treadle, so that a woman could work while sitting down (Figure 3). Instead of having just a spindle, the flax wheel had a more sophisticated mechanism, known as a flyer, that automatically wound the yarn on the spindle after the turning wheel had imparted a twist to the thread.

Many women, however, used an even simpler device, the drop spindle, which has been common in primitive cultures for centuries and has produced yarns of the finest quality. This sticklike spindle, which relied on gravity to make it work, was weighted at one end with a disk, known as the whorl. To use the drop spindle, the spinster held a bundle of fibers and attached the end of one of these fibers to the spindle. She then twirled the spindle as she released, or dropped, it, and continued to feed fibers to it until it reached the ground. Approximately one yard of thread could be spun on each drop of the spindle. Easily portable, the drop spindle proved a functional way for a woman to continue the task of spinning even while sitting outdoors or visiting with friends (Figure 4).

To measure and wrap the finished yarns into skeins or hanks, a niddy-noddy or clock reel (Figure 5) was used, although it was also done by hand. Much of the home-produced yarn was then sent out to professional weavers, most of whom were men, to be woven into cloth. Some weavers

**Figure 3** *Sketches of a flax spinning wheel and clock jack by John Lewis Krimmel. Detail in lower left corner shows the flyer mechanism. United States; probably 1819. From the Krimmel Sketchbook,* Book VI, *page 1. DMMC, WM, 59x5.6.*

FIGURE 3

**Figure 4** *Detail of a Boston "fishing lady" type needlework picture, showing the method of using a hand-held drop spindle. Polychrome canvas work in tent stitch, with crewel yarns. Boston; 1745–55.*

**Figure 5** *Spinning wheel, niddy-noddy, and hetchel with combed flax. United States; 1780–1840; Niddy-noddy from author's collection.*

FIGURE 4          FIGURE 5

also fulled and dyed the completed cloth, or the fulling and dyeing could be done by a separate concern. In either case, the cloth was then returned to the housewife, who cut it according to her needs for household linens or the family's wardrobe.

Because it took so much effort and expense to create even one piece of cloth, the basic wardrobe was simple and sparse. For a common woman, it might consist of a shift or two, a number of petticoats, a waistcoat, an apron, one or two caps, stockings, and a pair of shoes. Layers of petticoats were added or shed as the temperature dictated. The clothing of the men of average means was similarly basic—simple britches, often of leather, a few shirts, a jacket, a hat, shoes, and stockings.

Worn garments usually served as patterns when constructing new clothing. Only fashion-conscious women consulted the engravings published in European magazines, such as the *Ladies Magazine* from London, or sought sketches and directions from relatives and friends. For instance, in a letter written to her mother in 1797, Eliza Southgate, a Maine girl born in 1783, asked for patterns for gowns to be sent so that she could choose one to make a gown for herself.[1]

Sometimes a woman would make clothing for a fashion doll, or "baby." Some of these were commercially produced in England and France. The doll clothing illustrated in miniature a favorite dress or new fashion, and a woman would send it to a female friend or relative to use as inspiration for work on her own wardrobe. For example, in 1781, Rebecca Franks, a woman of means from Philadelphia, wrote her sister Abigail in Flatbush, "Nanny Van Horn and self were employed yesterday morning in trying to dress a rag baby in the fashion, but could not succeed. It shall however go, as 'twill in some degree give you an idea of the fashion as to the Jacket and pinning on the handkerchief."[2]

These miniature fashions were also created by dressmakers—or mantua-makers, as they were known—as a way to illustrate their designs to their patrons. In 1756, mantua-makers Mary Wallace and Clementine Ferguson advertised in the *New York Mercury* that they had "fashions in miniature" for both ladies and gentlemen.

After the customer had selected a design from the miniature forms displayed, the mantua-maker would cut the expensive silk and/or woolen fabrics chosen and fit the pieces directly on the customer. The final tasks were to stitch, line, and trim—often in a complicated manner—the garment.

Sometimes a mantua-maker or a skillful amateur seamstress would come into the home of a woman to cut out a dress. Then the woman would assist her by stitching the seams and hems. In her diary, Elizabeth Drinker, who was a member of a prominent Philadelphia Quaker family, mentioned that "Betsy Fordham sewing for us for the present. I have been busy with her for near three weeks, and am almost tir'd of confindment." Betsy Fordham was undoubtedly a professional seamstress who cut and fitted garments and did the fine work on them, leaving Mrs. Drinker to sew the seams. According to the Drinker diary, as the women worked, Molly Drinker, a daughter, read a novel to the older women, although novel reading by females was much criticized. Mrs. Drinker noted in defense,

FIGURE 6

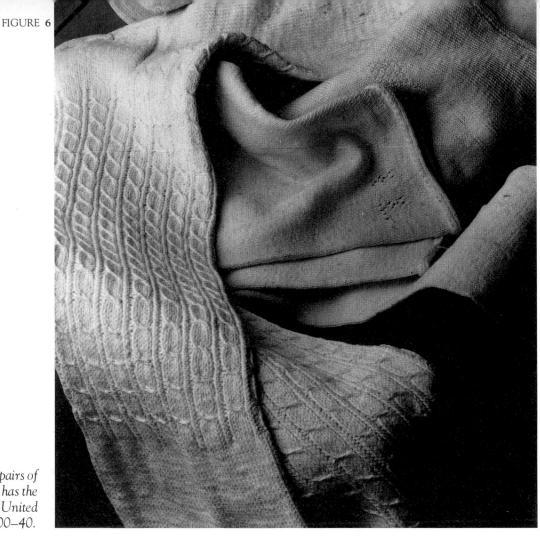

**Figure 6** *Three pairs of knitted stockings. One has the initials IL knitted in; United States; 1800–40.*

"tis seldom I listen to a romance, nor would I encourage my Children doing much of that business." Apparently, the tedium of this plain sewing warranted an exception.[3]

Young girls contributed to a family's plain sewing by knitting. Almost all girls—and some boys—learned to knit by the age of six. Stockings and mittens were always needed, and young hands could manage these simple but important contributions to the household well. The everyday stockings they fashioned often bore numbers or initials to facilitate matching them into pairs, which in a large family might otherwise be time-consuming. Sometimes this mark was knit right into the stocking, or it might be embroidered on in a contrasting color (Figure 6). For many children, marking was their first attempt at embroidery.

Like other kinds of plain sewing, knitting could be a pleasant task; once learned, it was so simple and mechanical that it did not inhibit conversation. Moreover, because it required little light, it was an ideal evening activity. In her diary, Sarah Anna Emery recalled with obvious nostalgia the fall evenings of her girlhood in Newbury, Massachusetts, when "the winter's stocking yarn was . . . carded and spun, and the lengthening evenings . . . [were] enlivened by the busy click of knitting needles." [4]

As she did her part of the plain sewing under the watchful guidance of an older female, usually her mother, a young girl began to understand the expectations that society held for a woman. Listening as she worked to her elders gossiping or exchanging news, she could absorb the attitudes and role expectations that would shape her later life. Here she would begin to grasp the implicit assumption that a woman must marry, even if no one told her so explicitly. As a result, most girls aspired to marry well and have a household to run for a husband.

In preparation for housewifery and motherhood, plain sewing was only the start of the things that an eighteenth-century girl needed to know. To later be considered competent, it was crucial for her to be well trained in the skills of housewifery. This training, which was sometimes her only education, was often acquired at home, from her mother, but some poorer girls were trained in other households as indentured servants. In return for food, clothing, and lodging, these girls, often as young as age eight, learned how to serve their new households in the various roles—cooks, housekeepers, washing women, seamstresses, and nursemaids—that they would later assume as housewives.

The practice of indenturing relieved a girl's family of a person to support, and it provided a more prosperous family with a relatively cheap servant. The arrangement was formalized in an indenture contract, which specified the parties, the term of service (the average term agreed on ranged between seven to ten years for girls), and the obligations of both the master and the young servant, including the freedom dues that the master was to pay the servant when her term expired.

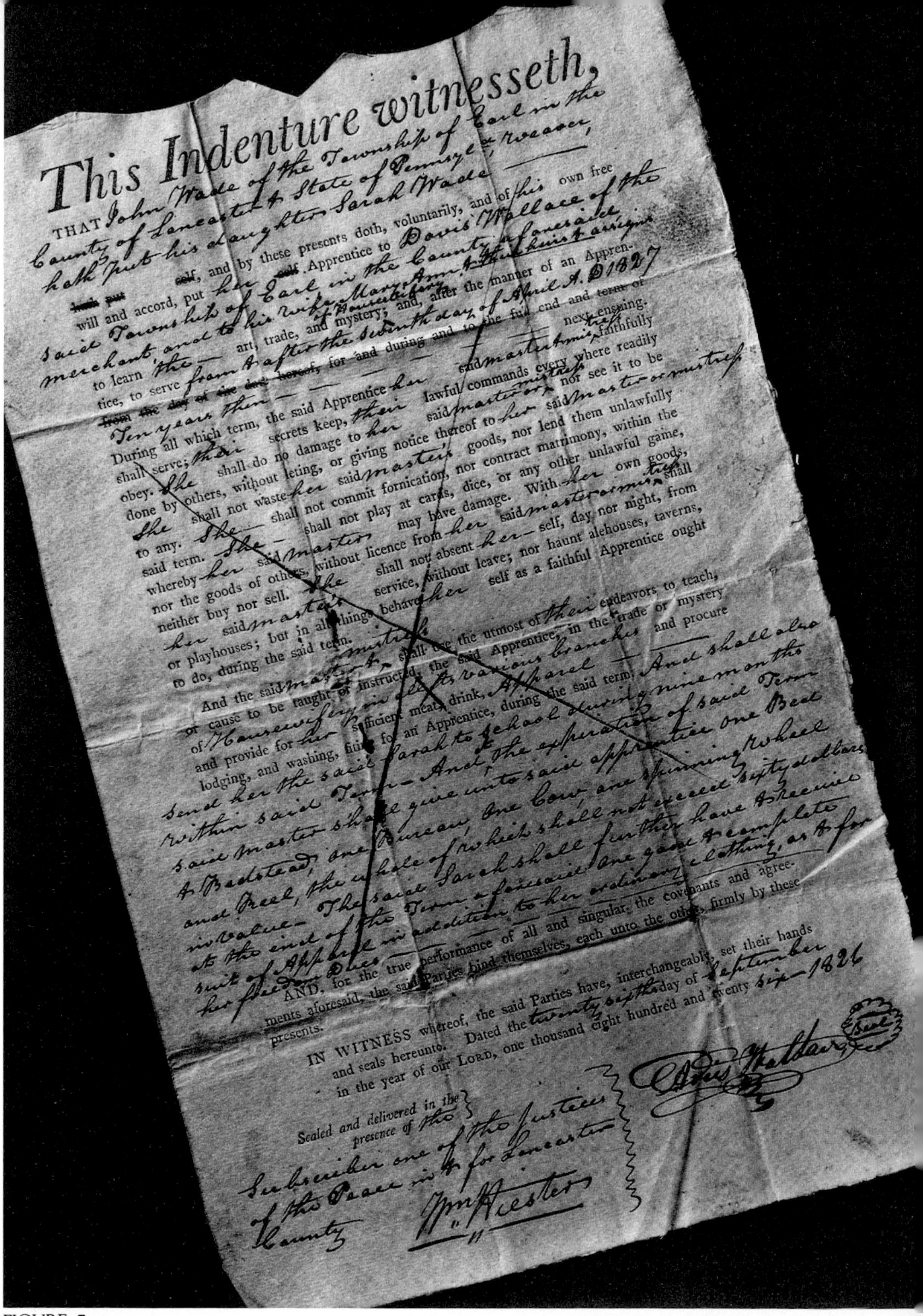
This Indenture witnesseth,

THAT John Wade of the Township of Earl in the County of Lancaster & State of Pennsylvania hath put his daughter Sarah Wade ~~hath put~~ and of his own free will and accord, put her ~~self~~, and by these presents doth, voluntarily, ~~self~~ Apprentice to David Wallace of the said Township of Earl in the County of Lancaster merchant and to his wife Mary Ann & their heirs & assigns to learn the art, trade, and mystery of Housewifery, and, after the manner of an Apprentice, to serve from & after the seventh day of April A.D. 1827 ~~from the day of the date hereof~~, for and during and to the full end and term of Ten years then next ensuing. During all which term, the said Apprentice her said master & mistress faithfully shall serve; their secrets keep, their lawful commands every where readily obey. She shall do no damage to her said master or mistress, nor see it to be done by others, without letting, or giving notice thereof to her said master or mistress. She shall not waste her said masters goods, nor lend them unlawfully to any. She shall not commit fornication, nor contract matrimony, within the said term. She shall not play at cards, dice, or any other unlawful game, whereby her said masters may have damage. With her own goods, nor the goods of others, without licence from her said master or mistress shall neither buy nor sell. She shall not absent her self, day nor night, from her said master's service, without leave; nor haunt alehouses, taverns, or playhouses; but in all things behave her self as a faithful Apprentice ought to do, during the said term.

And the said master & mistress shall use the utmost of their endeavors to teach, or cause to be taught or instructed, the said Apprentice, in the trade or mystery of Housewifery in its various branches and procure and provide for her sufficient meat, drink, Apparel, lodging, and washing, fit for an Apprentice, during the said term; And shall also send her the said Sarah to school during nine months within said Term — And at the experation of said Term said master shall give unto said apprentice one Bed & Bedstead, one Bureau, one Cow, one Spinning wheel and Reel, the whole of which shall not exceed sixty dollars in value. The said Sarah shall further have & receive at the end of the Term aforesaid one good & complete suit of Apparel in addition to her ordinary clothing, as & for her freedom Dues.

AND, for the true performance of all and singular, the covenants and agreements aforesaid, the said Parties bind themselves, each unto the other, firmly by these presents.

IN WITNESS whereof, the said Parties have, interchangeably, set their hands and seals hereunto. Dated the twenty sixth day of September in the year of our LORD, one thousand eight hundred and twenty six — 1826

Sealed and delivered in the presence of the Subscriber one of the Justices of the Peace in & for Lancaster County

David Wallace [Seal]

Wm. Hiester

FIGURE 7

**Figure 7** *A printed indenture form filled in on September 26, 1826. The father of Sarah Wade indentured her to merchant David Wallace and his wife, Mary Ann, of Lancaster County, Pennsylvania, starting the following year. The girl was to serve ten years and receive a total of nine months' schooling; DMMC, WM, 76x98.117.*

A very few girls were apprenticed to skilled professionals—mantua-makers, embroiderers, upholsterers, bakers, corset makers, or milliners—to learn a specific skill, much as young males were apprenticed to male tradesmen after they had reached the age of fourteen or so. But the greatest percentage of girls who were sent from the home to learn a trade learned housewifery, as of course did the girls who remained at home.

The roles of these young "housewifery" apprentices varied considerably from family to family. A late eighteenth-century Frenchman observed that in New England, where extremes in wealth were less apparent than elsewhere in the land, indentured servants were frequently the children of a neighbor or a relative. They were considered more or less equal in station to the children of the house and were treated accordingly, being allowed, for instance, to eat at the same table with the master's family.[5] In other circumstances, the typical indentured servant was more servile. Sarah Emery remembered,

> In most families there was a boy or girl bound to service until
> the age of eighteen. When the hour [tea time] arrived this young
> servant passed round napkins upon a salver; next a man or
> maid servant bore round the tray of cups, the young waiter
> following with cream and sugar. Bread and butter and cake
> succeeded only, these were passed round two or three times and
> the young servant stood, salver in hand ready to take the cups
> to be replenished. [6]

Not all masters treated their servants kindly. Sarah Emery also remembered a minister who bound and whipped his servant girl for slight offenses and, on occasion, contrived to tie her tongue to her great toe.[7] Unlike their male counterparts, female servants seldom believed in the efficacy of running away from an abusive or demanding master.

For any girl, indentured or not, marrying well was the best route to improving her social position. For an indentured girl, the chances of making a good match increased if she worked in a more affluent home, for there she could meet the prosperous artisans who did business with the family she served. To sweeten a daughter's allure to prospective suitors, many fathers tried to win a provision in the indenture contract for freedom dues that would serve the girl as a dowry.

One typical young girl, Sarah Wade, was indentured in 1827 (Figure 7) to a merchant and his wife in Lancaster County, Pennsylvania, to "learn the art, trade, and mystery" of "Housewifery." The settlement that her indenture contract called for upon completion of her ten-year term was a rather generous one: "one Bed & Bedstead, one Bureau, one Cow, one spinning Wheel and Reel, the whole of which shall not exceed sixty dollars." She was also to be awarded "one good and complete suit of Apparel," a provision that was rather standard for these indenture contracts.[8]

By the time an indentured girl had served out her time, she was presumed to be emotionally as well as technically prepared for taking on the duties of adulthood. Similarly, her teenaged counterparts who had not been indentured were considered ready to assume the obligations of a woman—marriage, household management, childbirth, and rearing children—all of which required both physical and personal strength.

❖ ❖ ❖ ❖ ❖

A pregnant woman would carry on normal social and work activities in addition to preparing the clothing and bedding that she would need for the baby (Figures 8, 9, and 10). When the expectant mother went into labor, the midwife would come to the house and stay until shortly after the birth of the baby. Despite the proficiency of the midwives, any complications during birth could cause serious problems.

Adding to the difficulty of childbirth was the lack of anesthetics. And women were often denied the few painkillers, such as liquor, that there were. The colonists had read in Genesis that God had promised Eve that "in sorrow thou shalt bring forth children" and, to the more literal, this was justification enough for denying women the minimal relief available to them (Figure 11). Cotton Mather, the famous Puritan minister of Boston whose career spanned the late seventeenth and early eighteenth centuries, believed that women in childbirth should have the same consciousness as anyone else in danger of dying. He wrote that a dutiful woman must prepare in happiness for birth, realizing and repenting her

**Figure 8** *Baby caps with cutwork lace inserts worked on white linen with fine white linen thread. One also has tiny, spaced sprigs, done in satin and whip stitches. Probably made by Deborah Hunt Jefferies of Wilmington, Delaware, for the birth of her daughter Ann in 1791; H. 5 3/4" (14.68 cm); W. 4 1/4" (10.80 cm).*

FIGURE 8

FIGURE 9

sins because she might sacrifice her life on the day of birth.[9]

An expectant mother could draw comfort from the fact that a physician would attempt to save her life at the expense of a child's, rather than vice versa, if it came to a choice. In *Outlines of the Theory and Practice of Midwifery*, published in 1775, English physician Dr. Alexander Hamilton stated that the doctor had a duty to give "perfect safety to the mother, who is always justly entitled to the first place in our intentions."[10]

If a mother survived the ordeal of childbirth, there was of course no assurance that her child would. The survival rates for children were grim. One in ten did not survive the first year, and almost four in ten died before age six. Such diseases as measles, diphtheria, whooping cough, mumps, and chicken pox often proved fatal. Eighteenth- and early nineteenth-century cities and towns were repeatedly visited by dysentery, smallpox, and, particularly in Philadelphia, yellow fever, to all of which the very young and the elderly were especially susceptible.

If a child survived these illnesses and some of the equally dangerous

FIGURE 10

**Figure 9**  *Unusual swinging cradle made of pine and maple, supported on a trestle base. Child experts such as Dr. Buchan considered the swinging motion preferable to the more vigorous rocking of a regular cradle. Interior painted mustard yellow, exterior blue green. One-piece quilt of French printed cotton, worked in running stitches in a pattern of scallops and diamonds; United States; 1800–30.*

**Figure 10**  *One-piece white crib quilt worked in running stitch plus accents of cross-stitch; wooden doll with white muslin dress embroidered in cotton satin and eyelet stitches around the neck; Pennsylvania walnut cradle with knobs on the side for lacing in an active baby; embroidered and shirred rug; all items United States; 1775–1825.*

cures, such as bleeding, other hazards and mishaps awaited. Elizabeth Drinker's diary records many instances: "A little girl of 6 years lost her life in a necessary [privy] into which she had fell. . . . two little children in ye Jersyes [New Jersey] some days ago, wandered out of their knowledge in the woods, and were not found 'till the third day. . . . one is likely to recover, the other not."[11] Two parents had "lost a little Daugh'r . . . between 2 and 3 years of age, she was left alone last night for a short time, and fell into the fier . . . she expired before morn'g."[12]

Letters and diaries written by individuals of all classes in both urban and rural areas often reveal a preoccupation with illnesses and a sense of helplessness in coping with them. Tuberculosis in particular, referred to as "spitting blood" or "galloping consumption," is mentioned with terror in many diaries.

FIGURE 11

FIGURE 12

**Figure 11** *Bible verse, sometimes referred to as "The Curse of Eve"; Genesis 3:16. This Bible was printed in Dublin, Ireland, in 1741.*

**Figure 12** *Signs of illness or death: a doctor's chest; a bleeder (the small J-shaped tool in the foreground); a silver pap boat, on the left; an early silver spout cup, on the right, for feeding invalids. It was common to drape windows and mirrors with black fabric when someone died.*

Although they took less of a toll in America than in Europe, with its crowding and unfavorable sanitary conditions, epidemics were common and the measures taken to combat them ineffectual. An enfeebled Abigail Adams informed her husband on September 8, 1775, that violent dysentery had already killed his brother Isaac and was sweeping through her household. Abigail had it herself when she wrote, "Our little Tommy was next, and he lies very ill now. . . . Yesterday Patty was seized. . . . Our house is a hospital in every part; and what with my own weakness and distress of mind for my family, I have been unhappy enough."[13]

With death constantly so close at hand, everyone—even children—learned to function while being continually aware of their own mortality (Figure 12). When Cotton Mather addressed himself to sick children, he reminded them to repent their sins lest they die soon. Unlike later revival ministers, Mather sought not to frighten them, only to urge them to prepare for the uncertain moment when they would face God's judgment.[14] But this approach might have produced more dread of death than resolution in facing up to it, since it was devilishly difficult to know whether or when one was spiritually pure enough to meet one's Maker. The threat of death could not be mitigated; it just had to be accepted. It was never too early to teach a child to start.

In this arduous life, children who were disciplined, obedient, and unspoiled were not only best prepared for coping with the rigors of life and the imminence of death but also best able to assist the family and the community. William Kenrick, English author of *The Whole Duty of a Woman,* warned mothers against showering their offspring with "an excess of thy love." He advised a mother to distance herself from her children not only as a means of lessening her grief if they should die, but also as a way of preventing children from becoming spoiled, indulged creatures who would "bring a curse upon thee and not a blessing."[15]

Perhaps the most dramatic indication of parents' thoroughly practical view of their children was the way they dressed them, which for those of average means, was unpretentiously. As young children, both boys and girls wore smocks or gowns, a fashion that continued almost to the twentieth century in many families. At about age six, boys were put into either pants or breeches like their fathers', and girls continued to wear smocks or dresses.

Before this changeover, distinct for boys, barely noticeable for girls, affluent families took to dressing their young boys and girls on special occasions in the elaborate attire of fancy ladies. At these times, such as for portrait sittings, the children resembled dolls, sort of mock adults, almost as if to emphasize their innocence and their protected status (Figure 14). But this upper-class fashion of womanly dress for little children had little effect on poorer children, who were likely to be dressed in whatever clothes were available and who were treated as adults as soon as possible.

English physician Dr. William Buchan advocated allowing boys to enjoy the loose gowns of childhood beyond the age of six. He complained, "Silly mothers are very impatient to strip them [boys] of their loose frocks and make them look like little men."[16] Obviously, this "breeching" was an important event for a boy. But for a girl, the shift from infant's to adult's clothing hardly mattered, since the difference was so slight. While a young male learned from his change in clothing that his adult role would be markedly different from his childhood one, a girl never fully left her childhood behind with the clothing she wore.

✤ ✤ ✤ ✤ ✤

The rearing of children added enormously to a woman's responsibilities. Although husbands usually exercised final authority in matters of discipline, mothers had the routine responsibility for looking after the children. They often found it a difficult responsibility to cope with. Esther Burr reflected after the birth of her second child, the famous Aaron Burr, in 1756, "When I had but one child my hands were tied, but now I am tied hand and foot [with two;] how I shall get along when I have got ½ dzn or 10 children I cant devise."[17]

In addition to bringing up the children, Mrs. Burr and all other mothers had a seemingly endless stream of household chores to do, many of which could not await the return of the husband from his shop or the fields. Routinely, a woman tended the vegetable garden, drew water, maintained the fire, cooked, preserved food, and cleaned. All these chores were in addition to sewing, which entailed a whole separate range of tasks.

pye from Bake-house she had brought
... it fall for want of thought

The ACCIDENT in LOMBARD-STREET
PHILAD. 1787 *designed & engrav'd by C.W. Peale*

And laughing Sweeps collect around
The pye that's scatter'd on the ground

FIGURE 13

Assistance sometimes came from other women—paid help, slaves, indentured servants, daughters, the family spinster, or other relatives, but few women were able to escape the household drudgery, and even the women who had servants or family help were responsible for overseeing the satisfactory completion of the work.

Few records illuminate the routine of daily chores. Most were so repetitive and boring that they warranted little space in letters and diaries, which in any case were usually written by the more affluent, better-educated women, who had servants to perform most of the menial chores.

Cooking was probably the single most time-consuming of the daily tasks. Basic cooking was held in such low regard that it was taught only

36

FIGURE **14**

**Figure 13** *Not all city women did their own baking. "The Accident in Lombard-Street" shows a servant who is upset at having just dropped the pie she was carrying from the bakery. The chimney sweeps and even the dogs seem to gather around to laugh at her. To the left, another woman carries home her pie. Etching by Charles Willson Peale, dated November, 1787.*

**Figure 14** *Portrait of a young boy, probably Benjamin Badger, painted by his father, Joseph Badger. He wears a blue dress with an orange red petticoat, and he is holding his pet squirrel; Boston; 1758–60.*

in the home. (If one could learn cooking outside the home at all, it was of a fancier sort, such as pastry making.) Women avoided as much of the basic cooking as they could, using children, servants, and even dogs to relieve them (Figures 13 and 15). Spit-dogs were a special breed of "little bow-legged dogs" trained to rotate the spit over the fire by running beside it in a hollow cylinder. One observer tells us, "As cookingtime approached, it was no uncommon thing to see the cooks running about the street looking up their truant [dog] labourers."[18] Some families purchased elaborate clock jacks to turn the spit. These worked with weights, much like a conventional clock.

Although clothes (like people) were washed infrequently, their upkeep did require some attention. For laces, silks, and other elaborate fabrics, there were professional dry cleaners, but the washing of everyday linens and cottons was usually a household chore. Elizabeth Drinker, married for thirty-three years, wrote, "we hir'd a dutch woman nam'd Rosanna to assist—washing at home is a new business to me, having been in the practice ever since we were married to put out our washing."[19]

All women had to learn to iron, a cumbersome and tricky task. To prepare the garment for ironing, the ironer first had to immerse the garment in starch that had been boiled until it was clear. To heat the iron, hot coals were placed in a removable tray in the rear of the heavy implement. As they expired, they had to be replenished. Since the amount of heat the iron emitted was constantly changing, maintaining the proper temperature took a great deal of experience.

To iron ruffles, such as those on men's dress shirts (ruffles were worn not only by wealthy men), a woman used a goffering iron, another awkward device. It consisted of a solid rod that was heated in the fire and then shoved into a hollow cylindrical receptacle on a base. The woman ironed the ruffles by pulling each of them tautly over the metal cylinder.

The daughter of a prominent Philadelphia Quaker family, Sally Wister gave some indication of the arduousness of ironing when she wrote in her diary, "Rose at half-past four this morning. Iron'd industriously till one o'clock, din'd, went upstairs, threw myself on the bed, and fell asleep."[20]

Thus, the early American woman was incredibly self-reliant and coped with great hardships. She performed dozens of household tasks thousands of times. Plain and fancy needlework were just two of her jobs. Quite likely married a little after the age of twenty, she would bear four to ten children and rear those that survived, all of this with great strength and steadfastness.

❖ ❖ ❖ ❖ ❖

As society became more prosperous toward the end of the eighteenth century, there were more and more women wealthy enough to avoid household chores such as plain sewing by passing them on to servants. If, however, a husband insisted that his wife do household work, his view

FIGURE 15

**Figure 15** *Writing on the rim of this earthenware plate, the potter Samuel Troxel ascribed this culinary credo to his wife: "I only cook what I can cook still; what the pig won't eat my husband will." Upper Hanover Township, Pennsylvania; dated January 20, 1846.*

usually prevailed and a woman could do little but resent the imposition as she submitted to it. Few women dared even to consider disobeying their husbands.

A 1792 issue of the Philadelphia magazine *The Lady's Pocket Library* includes an article in which Lady Pennington, an oft-quoted authority on manners, advised her readership, "All kinds of what is called *plain-work*, though no very polite accomplishment, you must be so well versed in as to be able to cut out, make, and mend your own linen." She believed this kind of mundane work to be the task of servants but recommended that if a husband insisted upon such labor from his wife—in his mistaken notion of frugal economy—of course she must comply. [21]

In the same year, a man writing an open letter to his sister in another Philadelphia publication, the *Ladies Magazine*, discussed the rationale for a woman's compliance. He wrote,

*A girl should be taught that her peculiar province is to please, and that every deviation from it is opposing the design of nature. . . . This state of subjection, for which nature has evidently intended the female part of the creation . . . makes it so necessary for girls to acquire a* habit of obedience, *and . . . makes* obstinacy *one of the worst faults they can possess.* [22]

One must suspect that it was to inculcate in a girl this "habit of obedience" that the man recommended: "A girl should learn needlework to perfection, but principally the useful parts, and though the *ornamental* be highly commendable, yet it must not be encouraged to the prejudice or neglect of the *useful*." He was speaking to (and of) the type of young woman who would probably not have had to do plain needlework unless her husband insisted on it.

Particularly for a late eighteenth-century woman who had servants or slaves, the everyday routine could offer such social diversions as card playing and tea parties. Plain sewing to these women could be a bore rather than a relief, as it was to the housewife who listened to the reading of a novel as a diversion from the tedium of seaming. As plain sewing became less necessary to survive, some women grew impatient with the demands of needlework of all kinds. They no longer wanted just to sit quietly and sew.

By 1837, a manner book, a form of normative literature popular in the nineteenth century, *The Young Lady's Friend,* felt it necessary to remind readers, "A woman who does not know how to sew is as deficient in her education as a man who cannot write. Let her condition in life be what it may, she cannot be ignorant of the use of her needle." The author went on to extol the spiritual virtues of needlework, calling it "truly feminine employment, a moral power which is useful to the sex. There is a soothing and sedative effect in needlework; it composes the nerves, and furnishes a corrective for many of the little irritations of domestic life." [23]

True enough, needlework—particularly plain needlework—could have a "soothing and sedative effect." But this reminder came just at the time when a few courageous women were beginning publicly to question the whole concept of woman as nothing more than a docile, virtuous, obedient, happy homemaker, content to sit home and sew. It was not so much the needlework itself that these reformers objected to but its symbolic demand that a woman stay in the home.

With the increasing industrial growth of America, men were pursuing their livelihoods more and more in impersonal factories and cities, and the home became revered as a family's haven in a harsh world. To maintain this refuge, a woman had to be there, presiding over it, ever available to minister to the needs of her husband and children. Numerous books and such new women's magazines as *Godey's Lady's Book* and *Miss Leslie's Magazine* glorified the female's involvement in domesticity and presented household tips and sewing patterns to assist and encourage women in their devotion to homemaking.

*The Young Lady's Friend* advised, ". . . decide upon what ought to constitute your daily round of occupations, and allot to each its fitting time. By having regular hours for different employments of the day, you will avoid the great waste of time." In a similar spirit, the book recommended that a woman sleep an hour less a night, calculating that in seventeen years she could thereby gain nearly four years of working time. The arithmetic was far off, but the message clear: Keep busy at housework; you belong in the home. And if, by chance, callers should interrupt a woman in the midst of her labors, *The Young Lady's Friend* had the time-honored remedy for preventing idleness. "Have a piece of needlework always at hand," it counseled. [24]

This advice continued to follow women throughout the nineteenth century and into the twentieth. Most women continued to subscribe to it. Even a pioneer like women's suffragist Susan B. Anthony saw no contradiction in taking her message to women gathered together to quilt, a favorite, sociable form of plain sewing that required a certain skill in making stitches small and even. Needlework was not the point of contention; Anthony had more important issues on her mind. And women began to listen to her message. It took nearly another century, but eventually women would be free to sew and practice housewifery more as a matter of personal choice than of social necessity.

# **2** Molding the Accomplished Miss

FIGURE 16

M atrimony. *Wanted, by a young gentleman just beginning housekeeping, a Lady, between 18 and 20 years of age, with a good education, and a fortune not less than 5000 £s, 5 feet 4 inches without her shoes, not fat nor lean, a clear skin, a sweet breath, with a good set of teeth, no pride or affectation; not very talkative, nor one that is dumb; no scold, but of a spirit to relent an affront; of a charitable disposition; not over fond of dress, though always decent and clean; that will entertain her husband's friends with affability and cheerfulness, and prefer his company to publick diversions and gadding about; one who will keep his secrets, that he may open his heart to her at all times without reserve; that can extend domestick expences with economy, as prosperity advances, without ostentation, and retrench them with cheerfulness, should the occasion require.*

*Any lady answering this description, and disposed for matrimony, is desired to direct to O. C. to be left at the Post Office in Savannah.*

*N. B. None need apply who fail in any one particular.*
—advertisement in the Gazette of the State of Georgia, *published in Savannah on July 1, 1784*

**Figure 16** *Susan Smith solidly worked her sampler of the First Baptist Meeting House of Providence, Rhode Island, while attending the Balch School there. The date at the top, October 29, 1793, and the "wrought" date of May 9, 1794, may be the dates she started and finished this work. Susan used both embroidery and canvas-work stitches, whip, satin, seed, Queen's, rice, tent, and cross. The silk threads are predominantly dark and light green with accents of brown, tan, white, and blue. H. and W. 16 3/4" (42.55 cm).*

Perhaps this advertiser was only joking; we don't know. But even if he was, his idea of the model bride closely resembled the ideal that well-off young ladies of the period aspired to in order to please a man. This would-be husband planned to be the center of his wife's world. He expected his wife to be not only competent but loyal, discreet, cheerful, and above all devoted. A tall order, to say the least. No wonder many a girl spent her entire youth and adolescence being cultivated to be a wife.

Even before a girl could grasp the assumption that a woman needed to be married, her upbringing was working to ensure that she would be. From at least the age of five until she married, her education consisted primarily of schooling in the traits that would make her appealing to a prospective husband, and a good wife and mother. These included not only the practical skills of housewifery but, as our advertiser above was careful to detail, the attitudes characteristic of a proper woman.

44

As she prepared for marriage and adulthood, a girl received an education whose quality depended on how close she lived to a school, the wealth of her parents, and perhaps most of all her parents' attitudes toward the education of females. If the parents' aspirations for their daughter were limited to finding her an acceptable match, her education was likely to be poor. And this appeared to be the norm. Historians have estimated that at the beginning of the nineteenth century, nearly half the female population in America was not literate, although most white men were at least functionally literate—this in a country whose general populace had the greatest abundance of material necessities of any in the world.[1] For example, Elizabeth Drinker, hardly a woman without means, in 1799 remarked with dismay that her nine-year-old granddaughter could not yet read.[2]

As a rule, education for girls ranked behind that for boys, which itself was unimpressive. Even in New England, whose Puritan population professed a strong interest in education if only to enable one to read the Bible, few areas offered free education to either boys or girls. In the first half of the seventeenth century, the Commonwealth of Massachusetts required towns of more than fifty families to found a grammar school, yet few were actually founded before the eighteenth century. Most towns found it cheaper to pay the fine each year for breaking the law than to build a school and hire a teacher.

In the South, fathers who could afford it might combine with their neighbors to hire a tutor to teach their children. Girls were usually allowed to participate in these classes for as long as their interests or abilities warranted. In some rare cases, a well-read father would permit a particularly promising girl to be tutored with the boys who were preparing for college. Or, an exceptional father might teach his daughter advanced subjects himself.

It was not until 1825 that the first free public high schools for women opened, in New York and the Boston area, and by 1870, there were only 160 high schools, primarily coeducational, in the whole country.

Boys training for a career such as commerce usually attended "English" schools, which stressed reading, grammar, mathematics, science, and geography. Boys studying law or for the ministry went to a similar institution, the "grammar" or "classical" school, which added Greek and Latin to the curriculum. Sarah Emery, of Newbury, Massachusetts, recorded that a girl in her area could attend the grammar school for an hour and a half per day in the summer—after the boys' session had ended—if the girl's parents paid taxes of at least three hundred pounds per year. Some years later the girls attended the schools from six to eight o'clock in the morning, before the boys' classes.[3] With such arrangements, a girl could not help but realize that even among the prosperous, the education of a girl was at best of secondary concern.

Among the very few exceptions to this indifference to the education of girls, Quaker Anthony Benezet, a mid-eighteenth-century Philadelphian, had perhaps the greatest impact. Periodically from 1754 to 1777, he taught daughters of the best Philadelphia families reading, writing, arithmetic, and English grammar. He also advocated education for black children and, for a short time, ran a morning school for girls.

✿ ✿ ✿ ✿ ✿

Before the age at which she might, if she were very lucky, attend a grammar school, a young girl might be sent to the early American equivalent of nursery school, a "dame" school, which for many girls provided all the formal schooling they would receive during their lifetimes. Not that the dame school was a very formal setting. It consisted of a small neighborhood class taught by one woman, the "dame," in her home. The pupils, both boys and girls, attended haphazardly and for widely varying periods. Some children began as early as age three, others as late as age ten.

The teacher made some attempt to teach reading and, perhaps, some "figuring," but for the girls at least, the most common activity was practicing the plain sewing stitches and knitting that they were likely to have begun learning at home from their mothers at about this age (Plate 4). These schools, which lasted from the seventeenth century well into the nineteenth, were essentially private schools, because the teachers were compensated by the students' parents in some manner.

Dame school was not necessarily a pleasant learning experience. Until nearly 1800, children were considered to be marked by original sin,

FIGURE 17

**Figure 17** *Print of "The Schoolmistress" of a dame school from* The Token, *S. G. Goodrich, ed., printed in 1830; facing page 295. DMMC, WM, AY11/T64.*

and hence this first training aimed at taming their will, stamping out pride and stubbornness. This attitude toward children had softened a bit by 1830, when a book entitled *The Token* published a nostalgic representation of a dame school (Figure 17). Accompanying the picture was a poem:

> *The hour-glass in its guarded nook,*
> *Which oft our tiny fingers shook*
> *By stealth, if flowed to slow away*
> *The sand that held us from our play.* [4]

The artist and poet here evidently worried little about original sin in these children. If anything, the children look almost angelic, though one notes a hint of mischief in the eyes of those not immediately under the gaze of the schoolmistress. She, drooping and bored, seems to have been a rather typical dame.

   After dame school, a girl might move on to a sewing class, again a small group taught by one woman in her home, but not likely to be in the immediate neighborhood unless the girl lived in a big city or fair-sized

**Figure 18** *Sampler signed "17&4 EliZabeth RUsh her WOrk done in the th year of her AGe." (Elizabeth purposely omitted her age.) Silk yarns in bright blues, yellows, greens, reds, and pink on a fine linen ground, intricately worked in cross, Queen's, satin, and whipstitches. This general design of sampler remained popular for another sixty years in the Philadelphia area, though later renditions of it were worked less skillfully. Elizabeth was probably the great-aunt of Dr. Benjamin Rush, a signer of the Declaration of Independence and an outspoken advocate of better education for women. Some of the verses are from* Epigrams on Progress *by John Hawkins of Boston. She also included the typical phrase: "This work in [hand] my friends may have/when i am dead and laid in my grave." H. 18 1/4" (46.35 cm); W. 13" (33.02 cm).*

town. The out-of-town girls usually stayed with relatives or friends of the family, but some boarded with the teacher's own family—an arrangement more convenient for the student and more lucrative for the teacher. Attending such a school allowed a girl from the country not only to learn fancy needlework, her most important accomplishment, but to widen her acquaintances among a new group of eligible young men.

We know from a 1687 letter written by Boston businessman and judge Samuel Sewall to his cousin in England that such schools existed even in seventeenth-century America. Sewall wrote that his daughters were about to attend school and asked his cousin to send a large supply of fustian and crewels for bed hangings and chair coverings to keep them "out of Idleness." [5] Undoubtedly, his daughters' school was a private sewing class for young ladies, taught by the local expert. Apparently, his daughters already knew plain sewing and probably some embroidery as well, so they were now prepared to do a large, expensive project under a teacher's supervision.

Schools that taught only needlework were very common in all towns and cities in colonial America. More ambitious schools, usually run by sister or spouse combinations, offered instruction in other accomplishments, such as drawing, dancing, and occasionally English or French. After 1750, the successful sewing schools began to expand, arranging for visits from teachers of music, English, and French. These were the forerunners of the true boarding schools, or young ladies' schools, that were common late in the century and through the mid-nineteenth century. Boarding schools were more likely to provide room and board for their pupils, though the town girls who attended them still lived at home. These institutions taught not only accomplishments but some scholastic subjects.

The early, one-subject classes were loosely structured, more like dame schools for older girls than formal educational institutions. The teachers advertised as private tutorial services—"at the house of Sarah Haigh," for example—not by a formal name. The pupils could be as young as eight or as old as sixteen. They stayed for anywhere from one to three years, attending class with varying degrees of regularity.

Twelve-year-old Anna Green Winslow, who came from Nova

FIGURE 18

FIGURE 19

Scotia to live with her aunt in Boston in 1771, seems to have been a fairly typical student, both in patronizing different schools for different subjects and in her erratic attendance. She went to Mrs. Smith's needlework school several afternoons a week, a dancing class run by a Mr. Turner (where she wore "black feathers on [her] head"), and a writing school.[6] Her diary discloses that she frequently skipped the classes, dissuaded by bad weather, feelings of ennui, or just the possibility of a more promising activity elsewhere.

✿ ✿ ✿ ✿ ✿

In needlework classes and even earlier, in dame schools, almost every girl worked a sampler, a piece in which she would demonstrate her needlework prowess (Figure 18). The sampler is one of the most intriguing forms of early American needlework we have. Certainly, it was a long-popular art form, practiced by the earliest immigrants and still produced well into the nineteenth century. It virtually chronicled needlework styles as they were changing, since the fashionable fancywork of any particular day invariably found its way into samplers. For example, when lacework became popular in the mid-eighteenth century, there was a concomitant upsurge in lacework samplers (Figure 19). Moreover, the sampler itself changed form gradually. The vague definition in Webster's 1806 *Compendious Dictionary*— "a piece of a girl's needlework, a pattern"—hints that the sampler was anything but a set form. The earliest samplers in America were not even limited to girls, as the dictionary says. Women also made them—quite intricate ones, in fact—as references of stitches and patterns. These early samplers were often ongoing projects, to which a woman would add another band as she acquired a new design or technique from a teacher or friend. As such, the samplers grew long and narrow, without borders. When they were not being referred to or worked on, they were rolled up and put away; these were not the display items that later samplers would be (Plate 3).

Loara Standish, daughter of Barbara and Miles Standish, made the earliest known American sampler. This piece is typical of seventeenth-century samplers in England and America in that it is narrow and long (seven by twenty-three inches) and displays a variety of horizontal bands. It also includes a bit of verse, not found in English samplers until the

**Figure 19** *In 1762, Sarah Keen produced this lacy cutwork sampler. After Sarah completed the circles and rectangles, she cut them away from the background linen and sewed them to each other. Then she also filled the spaces between with cut work and added her border. This small piece took months of tedious work. Delaware Valley; H. 7 1/2" (18.42 cm); W. 6" (15.24 cm).*

FIGURE 20

eighteenth century but known in American samplers from the start.

We also have a few written references to samplers that no longer exist. In 1694, Elizabeth Brunson of Farmington, Connecticut, willed her "white worked Sampler" to her granddaughter Elizabeth.[7]

In the eighteenth century, the form of samplers changed as they gradually became exclusively the learning and reference tools of young girls, eight to sixteen years old. These samplers were simpler, to allow for a child's ineptitude, but more lively. They became wider and shorter until, by the end of the century, they were often squares or wide rectangles. Many had a border, for these were finished products, meant not only to record but to display a girl's needlework skills. The girls almost always signed their samplers and gave their birthday or the date they finished the work as well (Figure 21).

Most girls from well-to-do families worked two samplers—a simple marking sampler, often done in dame school, and a more decorative, fancy sampler later. In the marking sampler, a girl worked an alphabet (sometimes her first encounter with it) in cross-stitch, as preparation for the marking of initials on linens and clothing (Figure 20). Then came the fancy sampler and/or a needlework picture, two forms that by mid-eighteenth century often closely resembled one another (Plate 6). Needlework pictures sometimes even carried names and dates, just like samplers. In such cases, only the alphabets and verse of the samplers definitely differentiated them from needlework pictures.

The makers of these samplers and pictures prized the works as being emblematic of the accomplished ladies that they were becoming. Most of the samplers and needlework pictures of the 1785 to 1810 period were involved projects that even a very industrious girl needed months to complete (Figure 22). Obviously, such a major project was a source of great family pride when it was finished. Parents selected particularly fine ones to be hung up for display, and the girls who made these pieces reveled in the praise they elicited. Sarah Emery recalled, "I became perfectly entranced over . . . [my] sampler that was much admired."[8]

Sally Wister, a Philadelphia girl, noted that a Southern officer (who was visiting Philadelphia during the Revolutionary War) "observ'd my

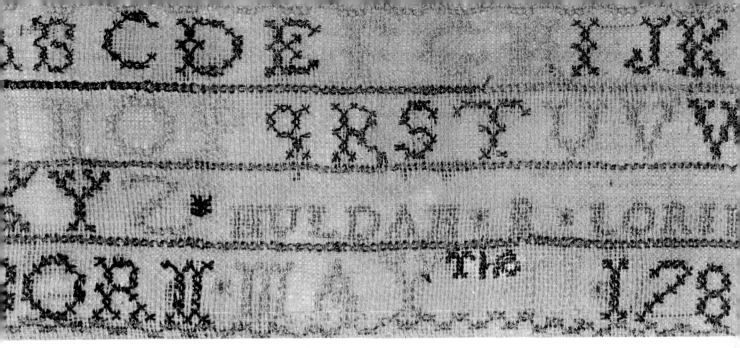

FIGURE 21

**Figure 20** *Hulda Loring even used the term MARKT on her simple, all cross-stitched marking sampler. Using a variety of colors, she stitched her birthdate, May 11, 1786, and the date she completed this sampler, July, 1795. Probably never intended to be framed, marking samplers such as this were kept in drawers and removed only for reference. Probably Massachusetts; H. 3 9/16" (6.66 cm); W. 8" (20.32 cm). Author's collection.*

**Figure 21** *Samplers from Mrs. Armstrong's school in Lancaster, Pennsylvania, were usually worked on very fine linen. Unfortunately, the sampler worked by student Phebe Bratton has threads on the underside connecting the letters and showing through the gauzelike ground. Her deep, flowered border of twisting vines sparkles with tiny satin, whip, and herringbone stitches. Phebe was far less skillful in painting than in needlework. Dated 1805; H. 16" (40.64 cm); W. 16 1/4" (41.27 cm). (Gift of Miss Elizabeth Hudson.)*

FIGURE 22

**Figure 22** *This ambitious sampler, filled with different stitches and motifs, was finished on January 2, 1818, when Elizabeth Andaries was twelve years and four months old. The lower rectangle is worked in diamonds of Queen's stitch; a central rectangle demonstrates her ability in herringbone weave darning stitches. Flowered vines worked in cross-stitch with accents of whip and satin stitches spring from cornucopias surrounding the arms of New York State and an American eagle. H. 19 1/2" (49.53 cm); W. 16" (40.64 cm).*

sampler, which was in full view. [He] wished I would teach the Virginians some of my needle wisdom; they were the laziest girls in the world." (This sampler is still in existence and is very similar to Elizabeth Rush's, shown in Figure 18.)[9]

As a woman grew older, her sampler or needlework picture became one of her most cherished possessions. She might bequeath it in her will, as Elizabeth Brunson did with her sampler, or present it to a favorite young female relative as a gift, as Sarah Wistar did with her needlework picture (Plate 5). In 1834, years after she had made her sampler, Mrs. Caroline Gilman remembered it with pride in *Recollections of a Housekeeper*. She wrote, "My sampler was one of unrivalled beauty. It possessed every shade and glory of tent-stitch. At the upper corners were cherubs' heads and wings. Under the alphabet stood Adam and Eve, draperied with fig-leaves."

With unabashed sentiment, she continued, "This sampler was a matter of curiosity, and sometimes ridicule, to my children; but now that they perceive my gray hairs and increasing infirmities, I find the sampler neatly folded and laid aside, and sometimes a conscious look reveals to me that they think I may soon be folded to rest in the grave."[10]

A sampler, after all, was a record of a blossoming young woman at the time when she hoped to become the center of attention of at least one man. If not always worked with the expertise she would gain later— though most of these samplers show true accomplishment—the sampler was likely to be charming, creative, and, perhaps most important  made for the maker herself. Most of a woman's other fancy needlework she made to adorn something, just as she as a gracious wife would ornament her husband. A sampler was her direct expression, and it would serve her the rest of her life, even functioning as a sort of memorial after she died. Jane Simons's sampler (Plate 3) reads,

> *The Gracious God Did Give Me Time*
> *To Do ths Work You See that Others*
> *Mayd Larn The Same When I Shall Cease to Be.*

Another sampler verse ended,

> *. . . [when] gredy worms my body eat*
> *In this you may read my name complete.*

Sampler verses, a virtual catalog of ideals that females cherished, show us the character traits that these girls were supposed to exhibit. There are odes to virtue, humility, selflessness, cheerfulness, and industry; dire warnings against the corresponding evils; and, as the two verses just cited reveal, an ever-present preoccupation, indeed an almost morbid fascination, with death. Over and over, girls began their verse with "When I am dead and laid in my grave," or some similar line. In an age during which, as we have seen, death could be considered imminent for persons of all ages, perhaps these verses served as a means for young girls to reconcile themselves to death.

Who selected the designs and verses to be used in the samplers is a matter of speculation. Correspondence still in existence shows that it was often not the children but rather their teachers or parents who suggested the compositions. *The Boston Magazine* for May, 1784, included three sampler verses written by a father for his three daughters. In 1777, student Nancy Shippen, a Philadelphia belle, received a letter from her mother, asking her to work a map sampler if her teacher had no objection.[11]

In their subject matter, inscriptions, and designs, samplers and needlework pictures show enormous variation throughout the eighteenth century. Many of these changes reflect probably nothing more significant than fads, started by one teacher and copied by others. For examples, young ladies in Philadelphia in the mid-eighteenth century worked fine silk-on-silk embroideries (Plate 7), while their counterparts in Boston at the same

**Figure 23** *This miniature canvas work of a shepherdess and shepherd is thought to be the work of Hannah Nichols, from the Marchfield-Hingham area of Massachusetts. It may have been her first attempt at a needlework picture. She worked primarily in tent stitch on the silk background with crewel yarns. She attempted some Queen's stitches, to depict fruit in the tree, and a few lines of whipstitch on the dress. 1760–90; H. 5 11/16″ (14.37 cm); W. 4 3/8″ (10.12 cm). (Gift of Charles K. Davis.)*

**Figure 24** *An accomplished rendition of a shepherdess, done in crewel yarns. The tent stitch is the main stitch, with lambs and tops of acorns worked in French knots. Notice that the spotted dog in the lower right is very similar in design to the lower left dog in Figure 25. The sky, faces, hands, leaves of some trees, and flowers are worked in silk tent stitch. A label on the back of this piece says that it was worked by Temperance Parker; undoubtedly she did it in a Boston needlework school; 1745–55. H. 13 3/8″ (33.99 cm); W. 16 3/8″ (41.05 cm).*

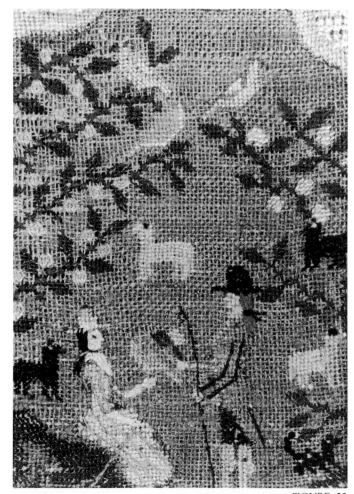

FIGURE **23**

56

time were working scenic designs on canvas in tent stitch (Plate 2; Figures 23, 24, and 25).

In the mid-eighteenth century, many samplers (Mrs. Gilman's was one) took to showing the Garden of Eden, complete with Adam and Eve, the tree of knowledge, the forbidden fruit, and the serpent. Then came elaborately bordered samplers and a craze for buildings stitched on samplers. While Nancy Winsor was attending Miss Mary (Polly) Balch's School in Providence in 1787, her father noted, "I wrote to Polly Balch that I could not send a Draft of a suitable building to put in Nancy's Sampler for we

FIGURE 24

FIGURE 25

**Figure 25** *Detail of Plate 2, showing a vibrant, tent-stitched, canvas-work representation of playful dogs.*

had none here [he was working for a while in Alexandria, Virginia], and advised to have the State House in Providence put in, for it is the best proportioned building I have seen."[12] This sampler was probably quite similar to the one done by Susan Smith, another schoolgirl at the Balch School. It showed the First Baptist Meeting House of Providence. (Figure 16). Map samplers (such as Nancy Shippen's), globe samplers, and darning samplers all had their fashionable periods (Figures 26 and 27). Genealogical samplers became very stylish late in the century, though some appeared earlier (Plate 8 and Figure 29). The late 1700s was also the time for silk needlework pictures that depicted floral, biblical, and mourning scenes (Figures 31 and 32).

Other sampler styles mirrored changes in the needlework schools, and even in the upper-class society these schools represented. When designs with buildings were popular, many samplers showed the school building at which the girl made her sampler. This sort of building housed a full-fledged boarding school, not a needlewoman's family and some out-of-town, part-time students. As boarding schools increased, so too did the number of samplers produced (most were made between 1800 and 1830), faithfully recording the institutions that produced them. Even if the name of the school were not stitched, certain distinguishing stylistic features might identify where the sampler was worked. For example, students in schools run by the Society of Friends characteristically used a fine, wavy band around their designs. True to the Quaker philosophy, these samplers showed meticulous workmanship and very conservative designs. By about 1800, the Quakers had begun to stress more academic education for girls, but they still required a perfect sampler of them (Figures 30 and 33).

✥✥✥✥✥

One of the earliest and finest of the boarding schools was the Moravian School in Bethlehem, Pennsylvania, founded in the early 1740s. Faced with dwindling enrollment from their own girls and increasing requests from outsiders for admission, the church leaders decided in 1786 to open the girls' school to non-Moravians (Figure 34). Daughters from some of the most prominent families in America traveled great distances to attend. They represented Lees from Virginia; Sumpters, Hugers, and Alstons from

FIGURE 26

South Carolina; Bayards and Elmendorfs from New Jersey; Bleeckers, Lansings, Livingstons, and Roosevelts from New York.

The school offered its students an exceptionally wide range of subjects for a girls' school of that era: reading, writing in English and German, arithmetic, geography, some history, a little botany, music, and drawing, plus intensive needlework training. A girl could enter the boarding school as young as age five or six and stay until she was sixteen. These many years of academic instruction were more than a girl could get at any other school in the country. Most radical of all, this curriculum was scarcely different from the one the Moravians offered boys (though in a separate school). The differences were that the girls were taught needlework and—because this early and prolonged schooling served as a substitute for home training—housekeeping. The girls could also learn spinning and weaving.

The town of Bethlehem became a popular stopping place for travelers interested in observing the Moravian life-style in general and a superior educational system. A prime attraction was the superb and distinctive needlework that both the girl students and the Moravian women produced and sold. John Adams stopped in Bethlehem in 1777, and later wrote his wife, Abigail, a letter describing the fine water system that piped water to all parts of the town; the best grist, bolting, and fulling mills he had ever seen; and the industrious women who spun, wove, and were employed "in all the most curious works in linen, wool, cotton, silver and gold, silk and velvet."[13]

An Italian, Count Francesco dal Verme, who toured America in 1783 and 1784, also wrote of the needleworkers in Bethlehem: "They make very fine tambour embroidery" [see Chapter 3]. The tour of the town conveniently ended at the shop where handwork was sold, and the count succumbed "to the custom of buying something, which everyone does who visits this place."[14]

The work of the girls was not always wholly their own. The pupils often paid teachers to add such finishing touches as the backing or stiffening to pocketbooks. In some instances, the teachers also supplied the designs. A typical entry for expenses, from a teacher to a pupil, was this one from Sister Maria Rosina Schulze to Betsey Dorsey, dated June 12, 1800:

**Figure 26** *A faded blue silk globe sampler worked by Ruth Wright while she was a student at the Westtown School. The longitudinal lines are couched in blue silk, the tropics of Capricorn and Cancer in red silk, the Arctic and Antarctic circles and the continents in white silk. The geographical names are lettered in black ink. Dated 1815. Diam. 16" (40.64 cm).*

FIGURE 28

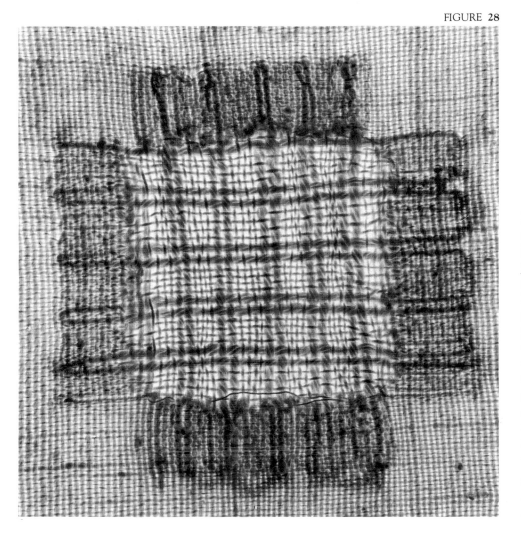

**Figure 27** *In a darning sampler, a girl demonstrated her skill at preserving fabrics—an essential and demanding skill for a good housewife. Anna Hofmann's darning sampler shows her proficiency at reproducing variations of plain and twill weaves. In the top row of squares, a variety of sample cuts have been mended. Pennsylvania; H. 13 1/8" (33.20 cm); W. 14 1/8" (35.80 cm).*

**Figure 28** *Detail of the center bottom square in Figure 27. Photograph by Ellen Lee Dwyer.*

*Betsey Dorsey ½ yd Sattin for a framing Pice—8 [shillings] 6 [pence]*
*drawing same—1 [shilling] 10½ [pence]*
*for making up a large Workbag—10 [shillings]*
*making up Pincushions—1 [shilling] 6 [pence]*[15]

The Moravian philosophy of education stressed gentleness and compassion, both in and out of the classroom. The teachers, or sisters, as they were called, were devoted to their charges. During an age when

63

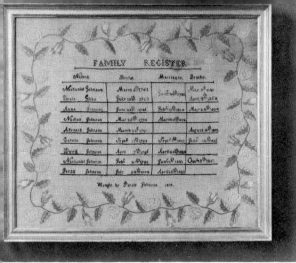

FIGURE 29

FIGURE 31

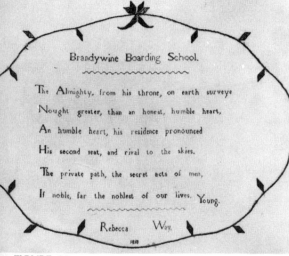

FIGURE 30

FIGURE 32

FIGURE 33

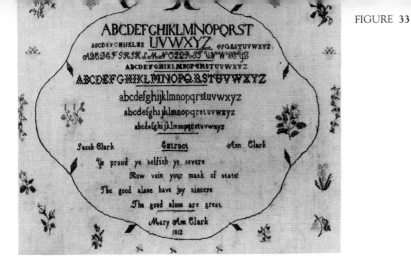

**Figure 29** *Family register done by Persis Johnson of Holliston, Massachusetts, in 1819. Worked with silk on linen in cross, Roumanian couching, chain, and back stitches. A penciled notation on one of the nine sheets of labels found against the backboard revealed that Persis's father paid $3.75 to Edward Lothrop of Boston to frame this piece. Another label recorded the contributions of Levi Lincoln and George Leighton, gold beaters, whose shop was just around the corner from Lothrop's. Undoubtedly Lothrop bought his gold leaf for this original frame from them. H. 19 1/16" (48.41 cm); W. 21 3/4" (55.25 cm). Author's collection.*

**Figure 30** *This wavy oval vine is frequently found in samplers from schools run by the Society of Friends. Rebecca Way attended the Brandywine Boarding School outside Downingtown, Pennsylvania, in Chester County. Her poem, from Edward Young's Night Thoughts, is worked in fine cross-stitches, the leaves in satin stitches, and the vine in whipstitches. Dated 1818. H. 11 1/4" (28.58 cm); W. 13" (33.02 cm).*

**Figure 31** *A family history glued on the outside of the backboard says that 18-year-old Mary Jennison worked this piece in 1773 while attending a boarding school in Salem, Massachusetts. Probably the school was the one run by Samuel Blythe, whose signature appears on the inside of the backboard. This versatile man was also a portrait painter, gilder, teacher of drawing, and an organist. The long, rather crudely done stitches using a distinctive crinkly silk thread on a black silk background appear to be typical of the Salem, Massachusetts, area. The same exaggerated scalloped skyline appears in samplers from Sarah Stivour's school, also in Essex County. H. 8" (20.32 cm); W. 13" (33 cm).*

**Figure 32** *Biblical satin-stitched picture, on a black silk background, of Joab slaying Absalom while Absalom's father, David, plays his harp, unaware that his son is dying. Absalom's hair is done with real hair and the faces are painted. Stitches are satin, whipstitch, and French knots. Salem, Massachusetts; 1760–85; H. 20 1/4" (51.15 cm); W. 22" (55.88 cm).*

**Figure 33** *Mary Ann Clark of Woodbury, New Jersey, attended the Westtown School when she made this sampler, in 1812. She included an exceptional number of alphabets, each of the eight in a slightly different style, as if she had copied them from a printer's handbook. Perhaps because of her proficiency in lettering, Mary was also allowed to include the stylized flowers —a symbol of achievement—associated with Friends' samplers. H. 16 3/4" (42.55 cm); W. 19 3/4" (50.17 cm). Author's collection.*

FIGURE **34**

**Figure 34** *An 1836 lithograph by George Endicott shows the Moravian church and the young ladies' seminary (in the right foreground) at Bethlehem, Pennsylvania.* DMMC, WM, BX 8560/T97.

birthdays were customarily almost ignored, these sisters celebrated their pupils' birthdays with "love feasts," complete with a small present for the honored girl. Likewise, the Moravians celebrated Christmas joyously while most of the rest of eighteenth-century society observed it more soberly.

To discipline the students, the Moravians would go only so far as to consign a disobedient child to the "unfriendly bench." The authorities threatened the incorrigibles with expulsion but only once had to use that extreme, as far as we know. By contrast, in other boarding schools, sewing classes, and even dame schools, corporal punishment was common. For minor infractions, the teacher might deliver a thump on the head with a thimbled finger. For a more serious transgression, the offender might have to stand blindfolded in the corner, balanced on a stool. Short-tempered instructors used switches.

While the Moravian schoolgirl was being intellectually cultivated and spiritually encouraged, the student at a typical girls' boarding school was learning the traditional female traits of docility, obedience, and graceful deportment. Teachers insisted that the girls sit with straight backs and heads held high while they studied or sewed. A staymaker, John McQueen, advertised in the *New York Mercury* for April 14, 1766, that he sold just the implement to encourage this discipline—"neat polished Steel Collars, very much worn by the young ladies in England, especially in Boarding Schools." A Wilmington, Delaware, teacher devised a cheaper method. She strung burrs on a tape and tied it around the student's neck.

At many schools it was standard practice for the headmistress to evaluate each girl's school progress and deportment in front of her class-mates. At Miss Pierce's School, in Litchfield, Connecticut, the headmis-tress reviewed the girls each Saturday. In 1802, student Lucy Sheldon recorded these weekly ordeals in a diary, which she, like many girls, was encouraged to keep to note her accomplishments and her shortcomings. She wrote that Miss Pierce "had seen no fault in me except holding my arms stiff, which made me appear awkward." The next week Lucy could write, " . . . [she] found no fault."[16]

The headmistress in the boarding school took responsibility for every aspect of a girl's training (Figure 35). Miss Pierce, an early advocate of physical exercise for young ladies, required her girls to take lengthy walks regularly. (By contrast, John Adams had found the Moravian women pale and unhealthy in appearance, probably from being confined in their efficiently heated but excessively warm rooms.) Miss Pierce also believed it was her duty to guide her students toward a Christian life. She continually conjured up the horrors of dying unrepentant and urged her students not to delay repenting, since they might die at any moment. Attendance at church each Sunday was required of the girls, and most of them diligently recorded in their diaries the theme of the sermon and the readings from the Bible presented during the service.

By schooling girls in character development, needlework and other accomplishments, and academic subjects all under one roof, the boarding school made a considerable advance over the one-subject classes. At boarding school, a girl was likely to attend classes more regularly, stay for a longer time, and learn more. Whereas previously she would have been lucky to advance academically beyond the rudiments of dame school, the boarding school gave her a basic academic education. In addition, it

**Figure 35** *Schools motivated students by awarding engraved school medals for good behavior and proficiency in studies. United States.*

**Figure 36** *A picture from an advertisement for the Andalusia Boarding School in Bucks County, Pennsylvania, depicted its healthy environment, far from Philadelphia and its periodic yellow fever epidemics. For $125 per year, headmistress Lucretia Chapman offered bed, board, washing, and a large range of academic subjects plus plain and ornamental needlework. French and piano cost $50 more, dancing $10. Her advertising stopped abruptly in June, 1831, when the school suddenly closed after the mysterious murder of her husband. At the trial, Pennsylvania's first for arsenic poisoning, Lucretia was accused but acquitted of spiking her husband's soup. DMMC, WM, 62x33.*

FIGURE 35

FIGURE 36

expanded her training in female accomplishments (Figure 36).

As the eighteenth century proceeded and the society grew wealthier, girls were taught an ever increasing array of such accomplishments. It began in the sewing schools, where a teacher would expand her curriculum of needlework or needlework-related techniques. All through the eighteenth century, painting and drawing became increasingly important to needlework; pictures done by reverse painting on glass were very popular household ornaments. Mary M'Callister in the *Pennsylvania Gazette* of June 4, 1767, said she taught young ladies the arts of "Painting on Glass, Japanning with Prints, Wax and Shell Work in the newest and most elegant Taste" as well as needlework. (She was also one of the very rare teachers who taught "Pastry" making, one day a week.)

The "Japanning with Prints" resembles modern decoupage work. Shell, wax, and quill work also found much favor with young ladies during the third quarter of the century (Figure 37). By the end of the century, parts of many embroidered pictures—faces, sky, and water—were painted on the silk background on which the pictures were worked. In the *South Carolina Gazette* for January 30, 1753, John Thomas offered to "undertake to teach about six young ladies to draw and shade with *Indian* ink pencil, which may not only serve as an amusement to their genius, but in some respects become serviceab'e to them in needlework." In other words, learning to draw and shade in pencil would have helped these girls to design crewelwork pictures or highlight their silk embroideries.

John and Hamilton Stevenson, limners from Charleston, South Carolina, announced their drawing academy in the *South Carolina Gazette* of December 19, 1774. They offered to teach "Painting from the Life in Crayons and in Miniature on Ivory; Painting on Silk, Sattin, &c. Fan Painting together with the Art of working Designs in Hair upon Ivory, &c." (Figure 38). The last reference is to the technique of incorporating a loved one's hair into a decorative ornament, such as a miniature or a piece of jewelry. Many schoolgirls practiced this craft in the eighteenth century, and it became increasingly popular during the nineteenth century (Figure 39). The Moravian schoolgirls at Bethlehem produced particularly fine specimens.

FIGURE 37

**Figure 37** *A quill-work sconce made an impressive piece of handiwork, hung on the wall in the home of a girl to be seen by prospective suitors. Usually sconces such as this were made of tiny rolled cones of colored paper, wax animals, and shells, then sprinkled with mica to catch the candlelight. A family history attributes this sconce, one of a pair, to Elizabeth Wendell of Boston before her marriage in 1733. Variations of this technique remained popular through most of the eighteenth century. H. 30 7/8" (78.42 cm); W. 14 1/2" (36.8 cm).*

**Figure 38** *A "print work" embroidered picture stitched by ten-year-old Mary Bowen. She copied from an 1801 engraving by William Rollinson, in turn based on a view by John Wood entitled "New York from Long Island." Foreground in silk yarns. Satin and whipstitches imitate stipple engraving. Ships and buildings in tiny seed and whipstitches worked with a very fine yarn, possibly human hair. The original frame and eglomisé black mat has a piece of a New Jersey Journal (Elizabeth) for March 24, 1807, glued to the back. Size of needlework only: H. 13 1/8" (33.27 cm); W. 19 7/16" (49.62 cm).*

French was another eighteenth-century subject that enhanced the image of accomplished ladies. Charleston schools offered it as early as 1739; because the city conducted important trade with the French West Indies, men learned French to expedite their business. Young ladies learned it to expedite their business of attracting men. After the Revolution, French became more popular in other large cities of America, spurred by our close ties with France.

FIGURE 38

A VIEW OF NEW YORK DONE BY MARY BOWEN IN THE 10th YEAR OF HER AGE 1807

All this training in skills and languages aimed at transforming a young girl into an "Accomplished Miss," as one schoolgirl, Eliza Southgate, called herself.[17] As the society grew wealthier and the boarding schools more elegant, the levels of sophistication that wealthy young ladies were called upon to demonstrate escalated. In 1853, one girl, Mary Service Steen of Philadelphia, felt unnerved at having to carry this worldly image. She wrote in her diary:

**Figure 39** *A box of hairwork, which probably belonged to a jeweler, with braided watch fobs and ivory ovals and circles for memorial jewelry. Young girls were taught to make hair ornaments and jewelry just like these.*

FIGURE 39

*I often wished I was sixteen; it seemed to me as if that time would never arrive but now when I have reached that venerable age I wish I was only one half of it. I dislike the idea of getting any older very much And to think of leaving school is the thing I like least of all. This happens to be my last year as a school girl. I suppose I will have to become very prim & precise; and in case I should not recollect or indeed not know anything about what a person is saying, I will have to appear as if I did, because I am a "finished lady," while now I am still a school girl I can show my ignorance if I choose.* [18]

It wasn't only Mary who suspected that a "finished lady" was little more than an ignorant schoolgirl with a lot of accomplishments. At the end of the eighteenth century, reformers began to charge that the boarding schools had become frivolous and impractical, and their graduates the same. Dr. William Buchan wrote, "A great part of the time [is] inconsiderately spent by young ladies in fancy works, and in learning to draw, to paint, or to play upon some musical instrument, of which they will never feel the want." [19] In Buchan's view, these girls were appallingly lacking in what they needed to know to be competent wives and mothers, and he suggested that they be trained in this field like any tradesman was in his. Buchan observed, "It is common to see women, who are supposed to have had a very genteel education, so ignorant, when they come to have children, of everything with which a mother ought to be acquainted, that the infant itself is as wise as the parent."[20]

Hannah More, a conservative Englishwoman, who did believe in better education for girls, wrote in *The Lady's Pocket Library,* published in Philadelphia in 1792, " . . . ornamental Accomplishments will but indifferently qualify a woman to perform the *duties* of life, though it is highly proper she should possess them" for amusement.[21]

These were the voices of moderation. They saw nothing wrong with the basic aim of the boarding schools, preparing a girl for marriage. They charged only that the schools had strayed from their purpose. Get back to basics, they advised. As Dr. Benjamin Rush said in criticism of teaching instrumental music to girls, "Their harpsichords serve only as side-boards for their parlours."[22]

As if to reinforce the charges of the critics, the needlework skills of some of the girls in boarding schools were becoming less expert. Beulah Purinton's showy 1812 sampler (Plate 9) demonstrates this gradual decline. Her green wool and linen background displays an attractive composition, but close examination reveals long, almost sloppy stitchery.

Some commentators went further than criticizing simply the performance of the schools. They attacked the very principle on which many boarding schools were founded. This was a time during which some women were taking very seriously the Revolutionary rhetoric of equality—so seriously, in fact, as to question the basic assumption that girls should be denied the academic training available to boys. To them the boarding schools were an abomination.

In July, 1791, in the *Universal Asylum and Columbian Magazine,* an article "By a Lady" (who evidently did not yet consider it propitious to publish her name) scathingly reviewed "the future education of girls." The article described a system in which girls were "committed to illiterate teachers, and as illiterate school-mistresses . . . are cooped up in a room, confined to needle-work, deprived of exercises, reproved without being

FIGURE 4

faulty, and schooled in frivolity."[23]

Eliza Southgate wrote, "I found the mind of a female, if such a thing existed, was thought not worth cultivation."[24] Later, she added, "Do you suppose the mind of a woman the only work of God that was made in vain?"[25] Of a Mrs. Wyman, whose school she had attended, Eliza said, "she treated me as her own malicious heart dictated."[26] However, Eliza had nothing but praise for a Mrs. Rowson, the headmistress at the second school Eliza tried. She wrote her younger sister, who was then a student at Mrs. Rowson's, "You must allow that no woman was ever better calculated to govern a school than Mrs. Rowson. She governs by the love with which she inspires her scholars."[27]

If all the fancy needlework and extra frills made for a frivolous education, not many of the girls seemed to mind as long as the schoolmistress treated them kindly. Sarah Emery remembered fondly, "Miss Emerson was a most accomplished needlewoman, inducting her pupils into mysteries of ornamental marking and embroidery. This fancy work opened a new world of delight."[28]

In any case, the criticisms of the boarding schools prompted the establishment of "academies" or "seminaries" for girls. Some of these institutions only used the new label and provided no real academic improvements. However, other schools made a genuine attempt to raise the standards. A few, such as the Deerfield Academy in Massachusetts, were even coeducational early in the nineteenth century. In 1821, persistent Emma Willard started the Troy Female Seminary (Figure 40) with four thousand dollars she obtained from taxes raised by the city of Troy, New York. Gradually, a combination of private money and public support helped such seminaries as Mary Lyon's Mount Holyoke academy and the Georgia Female School to raise their course offerings up to college level.

Even as women's education advanced, however, most girls continued to attend school to be groomed to win a husband and properly prepared to be his wife. The production of accomplished misses did not abate, though it did change somewhat to accommodate its critics, reemphasizing practical homemaking and providing training that was somewhat more academic. Following the lead of such eighteenth-century commentators as Dr. Rush,

**Figure 40** *A view of Emma Willard's Female Seminary in Troy, New York, from a woodcut published in 1841 in* Historical Collections of New York. *Author's collection.*

some nineteenth-century educators merged the idea of improved education for women with an already-conceived role for women as housewives. In his 1787 examination address to the Young Ladies Academy of Philadelphia, Rush had preached:

> *I know that the elevation of the female mind, by means of moral, physical, and religious truth, is considered by some men as unfriendly to the domestic character of a woman. But this is the prejudice of little minds, and springs from the same spirit which opposes the general diffusion of knowledge among the citizens [men] of our republic. If men believe that ignorance is favourable to the government of the female sex, they are certainly deceived; for a weak and ignorant woman will always be governed with the greatest difficulty. . . . It will be in your power, LADIES, to correct the mistakes and practices of our sex upon these subjects, by demonstrating that the female temper can only be governed by reason.* [29]

The issue was not whether to become a housewife and mother—that much was assumed—but how to be the most capable wife and mother.

By the mid-nineteenth century, housewifery was on its way to becoming not just the expected occupation of a woman but an exalted position for her. In 1841, Catherine Beecher, who had attended Miss Pierce's school and later opened her own school (it became the Hartford Female Seminary), wrote in *A Treatise on Domestic Economy*, "The proper education of a man decides the welfare of an individual; but educate a woman and the interests of the whole family are secured." [30]

Thus homemaking evolved from a dutiful performance of chores to a calling in which a woman could find fulfillment by creating a havenlike home for her family. Catherine Beecher, while glorifying the mid-nineteenth-century housewife, also gave practical advice on the best methods of accomplishing wifely tasks. Her advocacy of sensible, systematic homemaking helped generate a movement for better female education, and training in food preparation, health, nutrition, and household management. This culminated in the start of home economics training in public schools. Doctors Rush and Buchan would have been pleased.

Yet even as housewifery gained respectability and women were lauded for possessing "superior moral values," they could not escape being treated as second-rate intellects. As late as 1873, reformer and feminist Abba Goold Woolson could take the young ladies' schools to task for the poor quality of the education they offered. In the chapter "The Accomplishments" in her book *Woman in American Society*, Woolson pleaded that girls be freed from "the fancy-work which now engrosses their time and disfigures our parlor-walls and mantels." Needlework and "gewgaws," as she termed the other types of ornamental work, were "produced at the expense of the eyesight, the health, and intelligence of [our] daughters." [31]

At the start of the nineteenth century, Eliza Southgate recognized the intellectually stale life in store for her as a woman. She observed in a letter to her male cousin, "The business and pursuits of men require deep thinking, judgement, and moderation, while, on the other hand, females are under no necessity of dipping deep, but merely 'skim the surface.' " [32]

When she had finished her schooling, Eliza mused about "what profession I should choose were I a man." [33] She even went so far as to question the necessity for a girl to be married. She wrote, "I do not esteem

**Plate 4** *A simple marking sampler done by Polly Remington in 1799. Winterthur Museum also owns a stuffed and corded valance and bedspread done by Mary Remington (Polly was her nickname) when she was older; see Figure 81. Sampler: East Greenwich, Rhode Island; H. 7 3/4" (19.70 cm); W. 4 5/8" (11.70 cm). Irish-stitched slippers for a child worked in merino yarn. United States: 1830–70; H. 5 1/2" (13.97 cm); W. 2" (5.08 cm). (Gift of Mrs. George Lewis Callery.)*

FIGURE

marriage absolutely essential to happiness. . . . A single life is considered too generally a reproach; but let me ask you, which is the more despicable—she who marries a man she scarcely thinks *well* of—to avoid the reputation of an old maid . . . [or she who has] wisdom enough to despise so mean a sacrifice to the opinion of the rabble."[34]

But even such a rebel as Eliza Southgate learned to play by the rules. In 1800, she bought an imported piano for $150, though she admitted she had little musical talent (Figure 41).[35] Then she settled in to "patiently . . . wait till some clever fellow shall take a fancy to me and place me in a situation. I am determined to make the best of it, let it be what it will."[36]

Figure 41 *A fashionable Federal-style piano for a young lady. This one has an inlaid, painted, mahogany and satinwood case. The instrument was made in New York City between 1804 and 1814 by John Geib & Son.*

While a girl waited for "some clever fellow," she filled her dowry chest with all the necessities for a well-run household, including quilts, bed rugs, and the finest linens she could make. As she was thus busily engaged with her needle, she presented a demure, enticing female figure. Indeed the postures and attitudes of fine sewing exemplified the ideal woman—relaxed and at leisure, posturing prettily, her hands dutifully occupied, showing her industry. The stitches might have been difficult, but not to the extent that they commanded a girl's full attention. A girl kept her eyes downcast, on work in hand, but her ears and mind were open to the man paying court. She needed to be busy, so as not to appear too eager to be wooed, but doing fancy needlework was a pretty business, meant to encourage a suitor. In short, fancy needlework could be a sexual lure, a female ploy in the courtship game.

The sampler verse suggested by one father in the May, 1784, *Boston Magazine* put it succinctly, if discreetly:

> *And Man acknowledges, in all his pride,*
> *Needles attract, when our fair fingers guide.*

Gilbert Stuart caught this display of stylized femininity in his portrait of two young girls doing tambour work (Plate 10). Sitting properly and gracefully erect, dressed luxuriously, projecting the intelligence of accomplished ladies, these girls seem to invite a discreet flirtation. Certainly their needlework isn't distracting them.

PLATE 6

PLATE 5

**Plate 5** *This is one of a pair of perky bird pictures that Sarah Wistar, a fourteen-year-old Philadelphian, did in 1752. A piece of wool flannel was found under the silk; it served to shield the embroidery from the wooden backboard and pad it slightly. H. 9 1/2" (24.13 cm); W. 7" (17.78 cm).*

During the seventeenth century, when parental domination was more absolute, parents selected a mate for their child and made all the arrangements, such as provisions for a dowry and other financial matters. Usually the child did have the right to refuse to marry the parents' choice.

By the eighteenth century, the selection of a mate was still made by the parents, but also sometimes by the young people themselves; however, there were few places for the youth of rural areas to meet and to socialize. Church services, occasional barn raisings, and quilting bees provided some opportunity, but most of it was hit-or-miss, casual contact. In towns and cities, the parents arranged tight little social gatherings, such as tea parties, picnics, and fishing parties.

A socially acceptable method of bringing both sexes together was

80

PLATE 7

PLATE 7

**Plate 6** *"Elizabeth Richards Ended her Sampler in the 10th Year of her Age January the 10th." Unfortunately, Elizabeth did not add the year. The picture, worked with fine silk in tent stitch, is closely related in technique and design to the Boston fishing-lady (or shepherdess) pictures of 1745–55. In the lower portion, Elizabeth used real hair on the people, bullion stitches for the lambs, and satin stitches for facial details. In the sampler part, she used the customary cross-stitch for the letters and verse, and worked the border in eyelet. H. 17 1/2" (44.40 cm); W. 14 3/4" (37.40 cm). (Gift of H. Rodney Sharp.)*

**Plate 7** *Mary King signed this skillfully done silk embroidery in 1754. On a gold-colored silk moiré ground, she worked a sophisticated tree of life, accenting it with glass beads and detailing it with metallic thread. Mary used satin, whip, seed, and couching stitches for her masterpiece. H. 18 1/4" (46.36 cm); W. 24 1/8" (61.28 cm).*

that of dancing classes. Although Puritan New England prohibited dancing until the first part of the eighteenth century and the Quakers in the middle colonies also frowned upon dancing as a frivolity, the rest of the colonies had no such inhibitions. In the New York area, even in the seventeenth century, boys and girls of wealthy families attended dancing classes together. These classes eventually developed into even more structured and formal "dancing assemblies."

Once a young man and woman expressed an interest in each other, the fathers discussed financial arrangements. Generally, the boy's father was expected to provide about twice as much money or property as the girl's, but in areas where women outnumbered men, such as late eighteenth-century Massachusetts, Rhode Island, and Connecticut, the bargaining would not benefit the girl as much. A young man visited his bride-to-be after the girl's father gave his permission for courtship. Often the suitor had to travel great distances on foot, and under such circumstances long courtships were not the rule.

The man played the aggressor, of course, in this ritual. The woman appeared passive, modest, and virtuous (industrious), for which needlework was the perfect prop. In 1707, in *Instructions for the Education of a Daughter,* English author F. Fenelon wrote, " . . . beware of the Reputation of being *Witty;* . . . A Maid ought not speak but for necessity. . . . That which pleases in her is her Silence, her Modesty, her love of Retirement . . . her Industry for Works of Embroidery and fine Needle-Work." [37]

In an article reprinted in 1792 in *The Lady's Pocket Library* from his *Legacy to his Daughters,* English physician Dr. John Gregory added this advice:

> *It is a maxim laid down among you, and a very prudent one*
> *it is, that love is not to begin on your part. . . . (H)e contracts*
> *an attachment to you. When you perceive it, it excites your*
> *gratitude: this gratitude rises into a preference: . . . If you love*
> *him, let me advise you never to discover to him the full extent*
> *of your love, no, not although you marry him. . . . Violent*
> *love cannot subsist, at least cannot be expressed for any time*
> *together on both sides . . . [without] satiety and disgust.* [38]

Now this was a very delicate set of feelings to manage—gratitude rising to a preference but not to anything so dangerous as love. A girl had to know her protocol; propriety itself depended on it. Eliza Southgate implied it could all be rather trying for a miss, trained as she had been to devote herself to a man, yet unable to express it openly before he in effect authorized it by asking her to marry. Eliza wrote, "I would strain every nerve and rouse every faculty to quell the first appearance [of love]. . . . I could never love without being loved." [39]

There was plenty of instruction for misses on the theme of keeping up one's guard against suitors. In 1837, *The Young Lady's Friend* advised, "Never join in any rude plays that will subject you to being kissed or handled in any way by gentlemen. Do not suffer your hand to be held or squeezed, without showing that it displeases you by instantly withdrawing it." [40]

In his *Annals of Philadelphia . . . and Reminiscences of New York City*, John Fanning Watson gives us a glimpse of how this elaborate courtship ritual actually worked. Writing around 1846, Watson was by this time a senior citizen, who looked back with bemusement on one old courtship scene. He tells of a husband smoking his pipe while his wife,

> in her chintz dress and mob cap, was at his side, engaged in making patchwork; whilst lovely Prudence sat quite erect by her mama, with her pincushion and house-wife [a pocket, see Figure 56] dangling from her waist, and her eyes cast down, diligently pricking her fingers instead of her sampler. Courting was sober business in old times. [The beau] showed his affection very properly by keeping at a respectful distance. He passed the evening in talking politics and the scarcity of money with his future father-in-law; in assisting his future mother-in-law to arrange her party-coloured squares; in picking up balls of yarn, as they were respectively dropped by the maiden aunts; now and then casting sly sheep's eyes at Prudence, at every instance of which familiarity the aforesaid maiden ladies dropped a stitch! As soon as the bell rung nine, he gave one tender squint at [Prudence] and took his leave. [41]

One hopes that the scene itself wasn't quite as precious as the account of it. In any case, the American girls who engaged in these courtship rituals were apparently almost freewheeling compared to their European counterparts. In 1822, Frances Wright, the English visitor who wrote *Views of Society and Manners in America*, said, "The liberty enjoyed by the young women often occasions some surprise to foreigners." [42] She described American young women as "marked by sweetness, artlessness, and liveliness. . . . [They have] a certain untaught grace and gaiety of the heart equally removed from the studied English coolness and indifference, and from the no less studied French vivacity and mannerism." [43]

That gentleman from Savannah who advertised for a mate could hardly have asked for more.

PLATE 10

PLATE 8

PLATE 9

**Plate 8** *Genealogical sampler, or "Family Record," by Lorenza Fisk on a linen ground with silk yarn. At least four other samplers with this method of portraying a family are known from the Concord-Lexington area. Stitches are satin, whip, tent, flat, cross, and chain. H. 18 3/4" (47.53 cm); W. 16 1/2" (41.91 cm). (Gift of Mrs. Alfred C. Harrison.)*

**Plate 9** *Several American samplers are known that were worked on a dark green background, in this case, one of wool and hemp (or linen). "Beulah Purinton's Sampler ag'd 10 Danvers [Mass.] May 13, 1812" is cross-stitched in silk yarns. She used a crinkled silk, with satin, whip, French knots, and eyelet stitches for the fruit basket and surrounding flowering vine. H. 19 1/2" (49.53 cm); W. 15 1/4" (39.74 cm).*

**Plate 10** *Painting of Miss Vick and her cousin, Miss Foster, by Gilbert Stuart. Miss Vick is doing tambour work using a tambour hook with the material stretched taut on a frame. Her cousin holds the pattern for her. As they did tambour work young ladies could present themselves in graceful, beguiling poses. Painted between 1787 and 1792. Owned by Mr. and Mrs. R. Philip Hanes, Jr.*

# 3 The Golden Years of Needlework
## *The Age of Craftsmanship*

FIGURE 42

ost of the finest needlework ever done in this country was produced during the years between 1700 and 1780 by women of the more prosperous classes. The techniques they used included canvas work, crewelwork, and lacework, much silk embroidery, and, late in the period, tambour work. Most of these pieces were made to adorn an article of some sort, whether clothing, an everyday accessory such as a pocket or pocketbook, or—for the most ambitious needleworkers—a household furnishing. This was an age in which enormous importance was attached to possessions, particularly household possessions because people spent much more time in their homes than they do today.

A well-off man might occasionally leave his home on business, but colonial times had nothing to rival the transience of today's businessman. Most businesses, even excluding farms, were situated near if not in or adjacent to the home, and a man's commercial dealings rarely took him far away. Even a prosperous man was not likely to travel farther from his home than to a local inn or tavern to discuss the issues of the day and to enjoy some simple entertainment.

Normally, a married woman would venture out of the house only to attend church, to shop for the few household supplies she didn't produce herself, and perhaps to visit nearby friends and relatives. In general, it was not until the last quarter of the eighteenth century that the ritualistic tea partying, card playing, and other such lighthearted social intercourse became common among the women wealthy enough to have leisure time. Further, whatever socializing did take place during the seventeenth and eighteenth centuries almost always occurred in the home. Since there were no restaurants and little commercial entertainment, an afternoon or evening of recreation invariably meant visiting someone else's home or entertaining in one's own home.

During the seventeenth century, especially in New England, even most weddings were performed in the home, often by a civil authority such as a magistrate. As the eighteenth century progressed, ministers presided over weddings more frequently and more ceremonies took place in churches; however, the post-wedding celebrations not only remained in the home but grew more elaborate, fostering an even greater conscious-

**Figure 42** *A prim little basket of flowers in polychrome crewels sits inside a potholder's wavy borders. This potholder was undoubtedly saved for special occasions. Stitches are whip, cross, satin, and weaving. Dated 1773 by M W. America; H. 6 1/2" (16. 51 cm); W. 6 3/4" (17.14 cm).*

PLATE 11

ness of the self and the home that one presented to others.

With the home being the hub of social activity as well as of family life, a family naturally sought to furnish it as impressively as possible. Fine furnishings conveyed the level of one's prosperity and social standing far more strongly than they do today, because there were so few other indulgences and luxuries then available to the consumer for any amount of money. In an era when travel for pleasure was almost unknown, professional entertainment almost nonexistent, and the range of tangible luxury items severely limited, home furnishings represented one of the few ways in which a thriving family could display its affluence.

Moreover, fine furnishings could be practical investments. A handsome piece of silver, for example, could serve not only as a useful item and an object of display but also as a form of money. Such a piece was likely to consist of silver coins that the family had entrusted to a silversmith to be melted down and reshaped into an artistic form. The resulting hollowware was a more secure way to keep one's silver than in coin since there were no banks during colonial times. Furthermore, a piece of hollowware usually carried its owner's initials and some identifying mark of the silversmith who made it. If lost or stolen, the piece was far more likely to be returned than currency, especially since silversmiths commonly kept a suspicious-looking piece if it was brought to them, and then advertised for its owner.

Although not directly derived from currency, a piece of furniture could also represent an important investment for a wealthy family, and much time and consideration on the part of the head of the household would be given to the planning and overseeing of its creation. First, he would select a cabinetmaker and, in consultation with him, decide on the style of the piece, the woods to be used, the extent and placement of any carving or inlay work, and, of course, the price. Because fine furniture called for a fine room in which to display it, he would also require the services of a carpenter, a painter, and—for fashionable paneling and molding—a carver.

Fancy needlework represented a woman's contribution to the beauty of the family's possessions. Well-schooled wives spent months working stitched canvas or crewel-embroidered chair covers designed for the particular style of each piece (Plate 11). Some of these coverings wore so well and were so well cared for that they are still displayed on the furniture today (Plate 13).

The wives' needlework did not go unappreciated, for like young women's samplers, the pieces made for the home earned the praise and attention of all. For example, in his 1782 will, John Morris of Southwark, Pennsylvania, bequeathed to his grandson "8 Mahogany Chairs the Seats of which were worked by his Mother." [1] In 1820, another man, George Y. Cutler, reflected in his diary that when he had been a child, his mother and aunt "used chairs . . . which were 'worked' on the seat by their own hands. . . . [A] great deal of labor was bestowed upon [these chair seats] & . . . valuable and fashionable they were." [2]

Although it is impossible to tell precisely what sorts of chair seats these men were referring to, most of the chair coverings surviving from this period are pieces of canvas work (Plate 14). Often called needlepoint today, the appeal of canvas work to American women has always been strong. Unlike crewel embroidery, which apparently was seldom, if ever, done in the South, canvas work was done in all the colonies during the colonial seventeenth and eighteenth centuries. This colonial canvas work was usually characterized by four stitches: the tent stitch, the cross-stitch, the Irish stitch, and the Queen's stitch. The tent stitch progresses slowly, and before the twentieth century a needleworker could badly distort her canvas with it, since she worked it horizontally. It has, however, always been excellent for defining an intricate design. Occasionally, canvas workers used it in making pocketbooks, but it appears most often in work with detailed scenic or floral designs, such as the needlework pictures— for example, the "fishing lady pictures"—done in the Boston area during the mid-eighteenth century. The schoolgirls who worked these pictures did them almost entirely in tent stitch, usually on canvas with crewel or silk yarns. The chair seat in Figure 43 shows elements of the fishing lady pictures. Whether a schoolgirl or a more mature embroiderer did this particular piece, the maker obviously borrowed liberally from the tent-stitched needlework pictures done in Boston sewing schools.

PLATE 13

◀ PLATE 12

PLATE 14

**Plate 12** *A beautifully preserved Irish-stitched pocketbook with white basting thread stitched in an L-shape on the flap. This pocketbook carries its own written history: it was started by a young woman, probably in the 1760s, and left unfinished until 1817, when this same woman, who was then 73, remembered it. She quickly finished the purse (the part inside the basting) and presented it to her granddaughter, Elizabeth Titus Hicks, who recorded the circumstances of her gift. Mr. Anthony Saunder Morris, a grandson of Elizabeth Hicks, recently gave this pocketbook to the Chester County Historical Society.*

**Plate 13** *A finely worked tent-stitch slip seat, made specially for this chair by a member of the Bangs family of Newport, Rhode Island. This piece comes from a set of at least six, each with a slightly different design. The chairs marked IIII and VI are owned by Winterthur Museum; 1745–85; H. 14 1/2" (36.83 cm); W. 19 1/8" (18.59 cm).*

**Plate 14** *Irish-stitched slip seat with an alternating carnation and jagged oval pattern—one of the most difficult designs to execute. America; 1740–90; H. 14 1/4" (35.19 cm); W. 20" (50.80 cm).*

93

FIGURE 43

Since tent-stitched canvas work had a richness about it that reminded some people of the expensive and desirable loom-woven European tapestries, this particular style was occasionally called "tapestry work." For instance, a Margaret Taitail advertised in the *Boston Evening-Post* of April 23, 1739, that she taught "all sorts of Needle Work Tapestry, Embroidery, and Marking" (Plates 17 and 18).

Although women had learned how to cross-stitch by marking their household goods and the family wardrobe, they rarely used the cross-stitch in canvas work because it appeared rather coarse when it covered more than one thread (Figure 45). Only when it was worked over each thread of a fine canvas (Plate 15) could cross-stitch rival the tent stitch in the clarity with which it presented details.

The Irish stitch was by far the most common canvas-work stitch used during the seventeenth and eighteenth centuries if we are to judge by the number of surviving pieces and written references. No doubt its appeal lay in how rapidly it progressed and its facility, for it covered, vertically, three or four threads of the canvas rather than only one thread, as in the tent stitch.

Especially between 1740 and 1790, pocketbooks were a particular favorite to be worked in the Irish stitch. These small, envelope-shaped holders served in the stead of bank safe-deposit boxes, which didn't exist then, and enabled people to carry their valuables with them. Men used pocketbooks to carry currency, promissory notes, deeds, wills, and other important papers that they might not want to leave in a secret compartment in a piece of furniture (Plate 16). Women, who seldom dealt with legal documents, used their pocketbooks for jewelry, sewing items, and other trinkets (Plate 12).

The Irish stitch was also used for chair seats, the upholstery of easy chairs, wall pockets, pincushions, and even tablecloths (Plates 19 and 21; Figure 44). Elizabeth Drinker made a covering for a fire screen "in Irish stitch Flowers" (probably the carnationlike pattern in Plate 16).[3] A fire screen, when placed between a fireplace and a chair, allowed one to sit close to a fire for warmth and yet be shielded from the intense heat. Sarah Emery described one of these devices and its needlework embellishment

**Figure 43** *From a set of four canvas chair seats, finely worked in the tent stitch, depicting different scenes surrounded by similar flowered borders. Two of the seats are in the Winterthur Museum and two are in the Boston Museum of Fine Arts. The one shown here portrays a couple en route to market, carrying milk and fowl. Winterthur Museum also owns a silk embroidery on a black satin background with the same scene. Boston; 1740–60; H. 19 1/2" (49.53 cm); W. 23 1/4" (59.06 cm).*

PLATE 16

**Plate 15**   A cross-stitched pocketbook worked on canvas of 52 squares to the inch. The embroiderer chose to use crewel yarns and cover two squares with each stitch. An electron microscope reveals the red brown inked pattern guidelines. America; 1740–90; H. 7 1/4" (19.41 cm); W. 4" (10.15 cm).

**Plate 16**   Four Irish-stitched pocketbooks stitched in crewel yarns on canvas in the most common designs. The center right one is a "single" pocketbook displaying the zigzag pattern. It is signed HW 1760 for a member of the Way family of Chester County, Pennsylvania. H. 3 3/4" (9.52 cm); W. 5 3/4" (14.60 cm). (Gift of Miss Mary Swartzlander.) On the bottom is a flame design pocketbook with the name Nathaniel Green. An electron microscope reveals pattern guidelines only for a small area in the center. America; 1740–90; H. 6" (15.24 cm); W. 8 1/4" (20.96 cm). On the left is a diamond within a diamond pattern by Elinor Brown, dated 1753. Probably Delaware; H. 3 7/8" (9.84 cm); W. 5 3/4" (14.60 cm). (Gift of Mrs. Melva B. Guthrie.) At the top is an unsigned double pocketbook in a carnation design. America; 1740–90; H. 3 7/8" (9.8 cm); W. 7 1/8" (18.10 cm).

PLATE 15

96

as "an elegantly embroidered fire-screen, with mahogany frame, that could be raised or lowered at pleasure" (Figure 46).[4] Hand-held fire screens (Figure 47) served the same purpose less conveniently but less expensively and were considered to be important to protect the delicacy of a woman's complexion.

The Queen's stitch was the most difficult and time-consuming of all the canvas-work stitches (see detail in Figure 49). Because even fine crewel yarns were apt to fuzz so much that they would obscure the intricate nature of the stitch, the Queen's stitch was almost always worked in silk

FIGURE **44**

FIGURE **45**

**Figure 44** *A group of pincushions, each made using a different technique. These made attractive gifts and were a household necessity. The lower one, dated 1776 underneath, is done in the Irish stitch with crewels of red, yellow, blue, and white. Possibly Pennsylvania; H. 6 3/4" (17.15 cm); W. 6" (15.24 cm). The center cushion was finely knit in silk yarns by Mary Wright Alsop in pastel pinks, yellow, and green. Middletown, Connecticut; 1790–1800; H. 4 3/8" (11.13 cm); W. 3" (7.62 cm). The upper cushion is also canvas work—an example of silk cross-stitch. America; 1750–90; H. 4 3/8" (11.10 cm); W. 6 1/4" (15.88 cm).*

yarns. Usually it was limited to such small items as pocketbooks, sewing purses, pinballs, or pincushions (Plate 20; Figure 48).

Most eighteenth-century canvas work was done on canvas that bore between 22 and 52 holes to the inch, which is much finer than that commonly used today. The precise, careful work it demanded yielded an exceptionally fine quality of canvas work that demonstrates the patient pride with which these needlewomen regarded their craftsmanship and the importance of the objects they embellished with it.

Strictly speaking, canvas work is a form of crewel embroidery—that

FIGURE 46

**Figure 45** *Cross-stitched Bible cover made by Christina McCulloch, wife of Hugh McCulloch of Philadelphia, whose name is stitched on the inside edge. Coarsely worked over two threads in a brown red yarn, with polychrome yarn for the flowers. The Bible was printed in 1741 and the cover was made probably not long afterward. H. 14″ (35.56 cm); W. 10 1/4″ (26.04 cm).*

**Figure 46** *Original canvas-work panel in Irish stitch on a standing fire screen. The crewel yarns, in shades of blues and reds, are outlined in black. By adjusting the height of the screen, one could protect one's face from the intense heat of the fire without losing its warmth. Massachusetts; 1740–60; H. of screen 16 1/8″ (40.97 cm); W. 17 13/16″ (45.24 cm).*

PLATE 17

**Plate 17** *Pocketbook done with crewel yarn in the tent stitch on canvas of 27 squares to the inch. Though she carefully stitched each square, the embroiderer was sometimes careless about the direction of her rows of stitches. America; 1740–90; H. 6 3/4" (17.10 cm); W. 8 7/8" (22.50 cm).*

**Figure 47** *A shield-shaped hand-held fire screen of Irish-stitched canvas work in shades of red, yellow, blue, brown, and black. America; 1740–80; H.17 1/4" (43.82 cm); 11 1/2" (29.21 cm).*

100

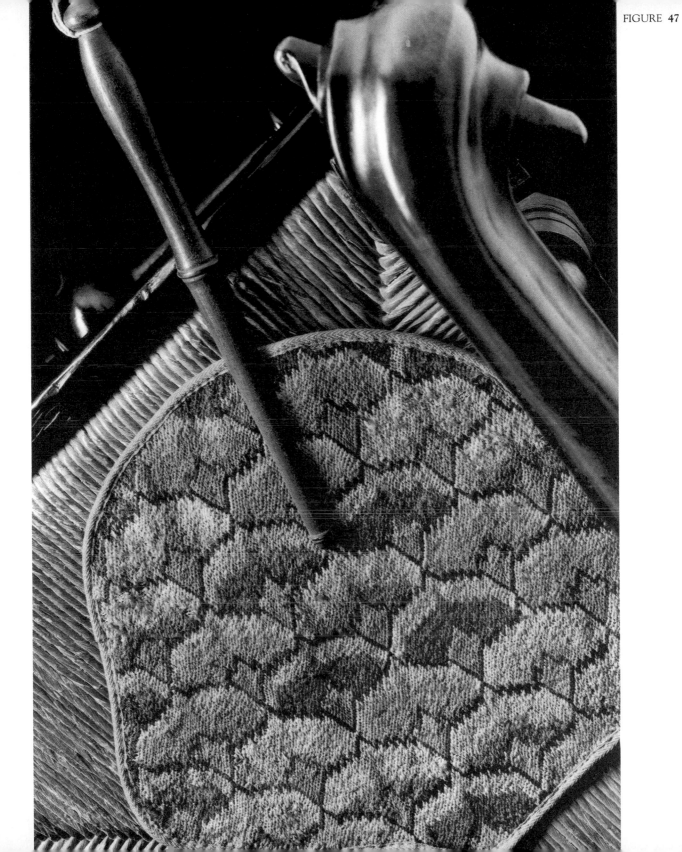

FIGURE 47

FIGURE 48   FIGURE 49

**Figure 48** *Pinballs worked in the Queen's stitch. One bears an attached chain, by which it hung at the waist from a chatelaine. Handmade pins and a silver needleholder. America; 1760–1800; H. 2 1/4" (5.72 cm); W. 2" (5.08 cm).*

**Figure 49** *Detail of the Queen's stitch worked on canvas in silk yarns. From a sewing case made by Beulah Biddle in 1783. Probably Philadelphia; 4 3/4" (12.07 cm); W. 4 1/8" (10.49 cm).*

is, when crewel yarns are used for working on a backing made of canvas. However, the term *crewel embroidery* usually refers to embroidery done with crewel yarns on grounds other than canvas, in which case the needleworker was not restricted to embroidering the specific threads as she usually was in canvas work.

To the colonial woman, the term *crewel* meant two-ply, slackly twisted, worsted yarns. Used not only for canvas and embroidery work but for knitting and even tambour work as well, crewel yarns varied from very fine (Figure 51), for intricate designs and stitches on delicate backgrounds, to fairly coarse (Figure 50), for such heavy grounds as blankets. Women who spun their own yarn could make it of a weight that fit their needs. Needlewomen who didn't spin patronized fabric and dry goods dealers, most of whom stocked crewels from England. In the May 6, 1754, *New York Mercury*, one merchant, Roper Dawson, advertised his London "Worsted Crewels in Shades." However, only if the family lived in a large port city or if the husband had business in such cities was a woman likely to have access to a dealer who sold crewels in different weights. In general, the

FIGURE 50

city woman had more needlework materials—a variety of crewels, silks, metallic yarns, canvases, and well-drawn patterns—from which to choose than did her small-town counterpart.

Although no pieces of American crewelwork survive that can be positively identified as having been worked before the eighteenth century, we do have evidence in the form of inventories that during the seventeenth century American women were indeed doing crewel embroidery to adorn their homes. These inventories reveal that people owned not only crewel yarns but also several varieties of linen and cotton cloth that would have been used as backgrounds for crewel embroidery.

In 1687, a letter of Samuel Sewall of Boston in which he ordered needlework supplies from London for his daughters specified, "white Fustian drawn, enough for Curtins, wallens [valances], counterpaine for a bed, and half a duz. chairs, with four threeded green worsted to work it."[5] The four-ply yarn Sewall referred to was a heavy yarn common to the monochromatic pieces being worked in England at that time. His reference to it suggests that the Sewalls were well acquainted with current English

**Figure 50** *A brown, twill-woven woolen blanket with strong designs in heavyweight crewel yarns in shades of beige, tan, blue, green, and red. The large stitches are Roumanian couching, herringbone, whipstitch, and French knots. New England; 1800–35; H. 78" (198.12 cm); W. 97" (246.38 cm).*

FIGURE 52

**Figure 51** *Exquisitely designed and executed crewelwork in three shades of blue. Very fine crewel yarns are stitched in an unusually great variety of stitches: Roumanian couching, whip, back, herringbone, seed, satin, buttonhole, cross, and weaving. Not in its original form and quilted at a later date. Massachusetts; 1740–80; H. 90 1/2" (229.87 cm); W. 96 1/4" (244.47 cm).*

**Figure 52** *A small section of a design that repeats itself every 49 inches on various parts of a multipiece crewel and silk bedhanging. The background fabric is a cotton and linen dimity. The predominant stitch is the customary American one, Roumanian couching. (It is worked in exceptional fineness—48 to 50 stitches to the inch with the rows less than one-eighth inch high.) The meticulous workmanship suggests a professional embroiderer, but the origin of these pieces cannot be clearly traced. Long known as the Penn hangings, they are said to have been purchased by Walter Stewart at the sale of John Penn's belongings in 1788. However, no specific mention of embroidered hangings appears in Penn's inventory for the sale. John Watson commented in his Annals of Philadelphia, that "he preserved a piece of bed cover worked by....." Letitia Penn (William Penn's daughter). England or America; 1680–1740.*

embroidery fashions, and they apparently thought well of them. Sewall wanted not only the fashionable crewels but probably matching designs for all the pieces, ready for working. The fact that Sewall ordered everything at once is again typical. Colonists preferred coordinated interiors and usually decorated an entire room with just one fabric —calling each room by its predominant color. In this case, Sewall was ordering for "the green room." Fustian was a twill-woven fabric, usually of a cotton weft on a linen warp but occasionally all cotton. Surviving early crewelwork and early written references show a preference for backgrounds of either fustian or dimity. Dimity differed from fustian in its fine, vertical ribs and tufting that resembles today's finest corduroy (Figure 52). (Fustian and dimity were sometimes confused. Webster's 1806 *Compendious Dictionary* defined dimity

FIGURE 51

105

as "a kind of white fustian, a fine fustian.") Although dimity and fustian were both used in American crewelwork, plain-woven linen backgrounds predominate.

While patterns could be ordered from England as the Sewalls did, unless she were especially talented, a woman usually prevailed upon someone else to do the designs for her. Often it was a friend or relative known for his or her artistic abilities. Sarah Emery mentioned that her Aunt Sarah "drew a lively vine of roses and leaves" for her skirt (Plate 23).[6] Lacking such local amateur talent, the embroiderer would turn to a professional. But even those who advertised skill at embroidery designing

FIGURE 53

FIGURE 54

**Figure 53** *Large canvas-work piece exhibits extremely uneven and generally poor workmanship. Silk, wool, and cotton yarns have been used in cross, satin, and whipstitches. Boston area; 1745–60; H. 32" (81.28 cm); W. 59 1/4" (150.50 cm).*

**Figure 54** *Multicolored side panel graced by an undulating flower vine and five fanciful birds flitting through it. Shelburne Museum in Shelburne, Vermont, owns a piece with a very similar design. The stitches are flat, whip, back, satin, buttonhole, bullion, weaving, and herringbone. Probably Massachusetts; 1750–1800; H. 70 1/2" (179.07 cm); W. 33" (83.82 cm).*

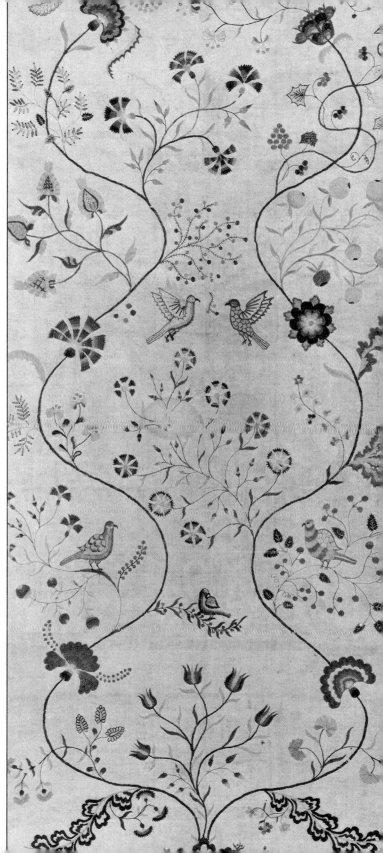

often plied other occupations, as diverse as portrait painter, engraver, tailor, chaise and harness maker, and, of course, art and needlework teacher.

When it came to filling in the design, for the most part a woman chose her own stitches. Unfinished pieces on which the inked drawings are still visible show not only a design outline, but occasionally marks that are suggestive of a stitch, such as dots for French knots or seed stitches (Plate 22). By determining herself whether a particular area would be made light and open with spaced seed stitches, have the prickly edge of the buttonhole stitch, or be a strong, positive area worked in a solid stitch like Roumanian couching, a woman could turn someone else's design into her own unique needlework creation. The choice of colors to be used was also the embroiderer's province, and color "shading" was taught to girls in needlework classes.

When looking at the needlework pieces, it is important to remember that at this time creativity meant something quite different from what it means today. Artists were expected to adhere to rather strictly defined forms, in which they demonstrated their proficiency first, and only second their originality. They often used copy work to perfect their techniques; even well-known American artists copied poses and background features from European prints. A needleworker merited less praise for producing an inferior original design than for tracing or copying a superior one. She preferred to use her creativity in interpreting the design with the stitches and colors that best displayed her craftsmanship (Plate 26 and Figure 54).

While any girl or woman could purchase an attractive pattern, skilled instruction, and proper materials, not every woman could produce a pleasing product. Unfortunately for them, a minority of women found needlework distasteful and yet unavoidable in a female's social role (Figure 53). However, the pieces that exhibit a special exuberance and originality signify that some embroiderers must have known great joy in their work (Plate 29).

The society that prized beautiful material possessions quite naturally demanded fine craftsmanship. Although artisans in the colonies were spared the rigid guild system still functioning in Europe at this time, long training and practice were still required of them. Apprenticeship periods of five to seven years produced skilled, meticulously trained craftsmen. Seen in this context, the many years a girl spent mastering the intricacies of fancy sewing, often at the expense of any intellectual training, represented an investment in her artistic talents, not only a failure to appreciate her intellectual possibilities. Though this age was hardly free of cultural snobbery, there was a minimum of pretension. People who had little or no education took pride in the fine work they did with their hands because society valued their contributions. It was an age for the appreciation of fine workmanship and the unaffected display of it (Plate 24).

Sometimes, the display of fine work took precedence over thoroughness. Cabinetmakers who customarily lavished great attention and care on the front and sides of a fine piece of furniture saw nothing wrong with ignoring the parts that didn't show. They didn't stain or even sand the backs of pieces or the bottoms of drawers, only planing those surfaces and sometimes leaving them rough enough to produce splinters. Similarly, the most exquisitely done needlework surfaces often gave no hint of the clumsy knots and long, untidy stitches on the back. Not until the Victorian Age and its fastidious concern for appearances would this sort of needlework be considered unaccomplished. Then, even the back was expected to be neat.

The demand for fine embroidery and the esteem such work commanded were so great that a few professional male embroiderers established themselves in the larger American cities. Although some of these men called themselves tailors and used their embroidery skills to work fancy buttonholes and trim (for both men and women), others plainly identified themselves as embroiderers. In England and parts of the Continent, professional embroiderers (mostly male) were well known, respected, and highly influential over amateur needleworkers (mostly female). Levy Simons, who advertised periodically in New York City for at least twenty-three years, had probably once been a member of the English Embroiderers Guild, incorporated in 1561 and still active in the eighteenth century. He never failed to refer to himself as an "Embroider from LONDON," even after he had become well established in the colonies. In the *New York*

*Mercury* of October 9, 1758, he gave some indication of the diverse skills of an accomplished professional embroiderer. He advertised that he worked "in Gold or Silver, shading in Silk or Worsted work'd Robins, Facings, Handkerchiefs, Aprons or Shoes, Dresden Work of all sorts, done in the neatest and newest Fashion." In addition, Simons removed spots from and cleaned silk, drew patterns, and, by 1777, had added tambour work to his repertoire.

The use of stitches in American crewelwork varied from that of English pieces. In England an example of fine crewelwork often contained twenty or more different stitches, probably because of the influence of the Embroiderers Guild with its rigid standards. American work usually used only four to seven different stitches, even for large pieces. Here, the solidly embroidered areas were usually worked in the stitch known as Roumanian couching, Oriental stitch, or crewel stitch (Figure 55). Unfortunately, the colonial terms for this stitch, and a very similar one now called the flat or New England laid stitch, elude us. We do know that Roumanian

FIGURE 55

**Figure 55** *Unlined crewelwork valance in four shades of blue. It shows how solidly the Roumanian couching stitch appears on the surface and its sparseness underneath. The disregard for neatness on the reverse side is noticeable. Other stitches are buttonhole, whip, herringbone, and cross. New England; 1730–70; H. 10" (25.30 cm); W. 71 1/2" (181.60 cm).*

110

couching and flat stitch occurred far more frequently in American work than in English work. English women usually worked solidly embroidered areas in the satin stitch, or its variation, the long and short stitch. The work progressed slightly more slowly and was harder to control, but the result was shinier.

Certain regional preferences show up in crewelwork. Large projects such as bed hangings do not seem to have been done in Pennsylvania, where women chose to do small items, such as pictures (Plate 25) and pot holders, or "Tea Kittle Holders," as Elizabeth Drinker called them (Figure 42).

From New England come many charming petticoat borders (Plates 22 and 27), a few needlework pictures (usually similar to the canvas-worked ones), and slip seat covers (Plate 28). Women's pockets, usually worn in pairs, were attached to a tape that was tied around the waist, so that there was a pocket on each hip (Figure 56). Even when these pockets were worn under the outer skirt, they were often ornamented in crewel or canvas work. Fortunately, fashion approved of the bulky profile that resulted from a woman carrying things like her sewing, keys, and even her pocketbook in these colonial pockets.

The English influence is most apparent in the American crewelwork done in the Boston area, with its more precise and formal stitchery and use of delicate, well-proportioned flowers. No doubt much of the Bostonian crewelwork was done under the supervision or influence of teachers familiar with English Queen Anne crewelwork.

In the more isolated areas of the colonies, indigenous styles developed. Women in Deerfield, Massachusetts, for instance, produced many pieces in monochromatic blues (probably dyed by the needleworkers themselves). These Deerfield pieces have a characteristically prickly appearance resulting from many of the edgings having been done in the buttonhole stitch. In general, they show a preference for rather open designs with few solidly embroidered areas (Figure 57).

The only known crewelwork dresses seem to have originated in Connecticut. Connecticut crewelwork, similar to the region's furniture, was freely designed, flamboyant, and innovative (Figure 58). Large, exotic flowers, often topping stems so wide that they needed an inner band of

design (Plate 30), were often used. Toward the end of the crewelwork era, crewel-embroidered pieces from the Connecticut River Valley included a number of vibrantly designed woolen blankets (Figure 50). The large-scale, bold designs that they bore were usually worked in proportionately heavier crewel yarns.

Of all the items ornamented with crewelwork embroidery, bed hangings presented the most dramatic display—and challenge. Only a woman with great diligence, willing to invest several years of stitchery, would launch such a project, a project calling for the preparation of countless yards of fabric and hanks of yarn before the embroidery could even be started. Because until almost the mid-eighteenth century, many families—even large ones—lived in houses of only three to five rooms, rooms had to serve several purposes. As a result, the master bed frequently found itself in the parlor. Since the parlor was also the "company" room, where family visits and teas were held, it was incumbent upon a woman

FIGURE 57

**Figure 56** *Crewel-embroidered pair of pockets dated 1777 by MM. Stitches are satin, whip, bullion, buttonhole, and French knots. America; H. 18 1/2" (46.99 cm); W. 12 3/8" (31.45 cm). The pockets are shown against a dark olive green silk one-piece petticoat with a beige glazed wool lining. H. 32 1/4" (81.91 cm).*

**Figure 57** *Three crewelwork valances. The top one, with its central cherry tree, is shaped as it was originally cut and has a tiny rolled hem on the edges. It features an unusual color scheme for crewelwork: orange red, brown, yellows, greens, gray, and beiges. It is stitched in herringbone, satin, whip, and cross-stitches. New England; 1725–75; H. 8 3/4" (22.20 cm); W. 56 1/2" (143.50 cm). The center valance, worked in two shades of blue, with few solid areas, is typical of the distinctive crewelwork done in the Deerfield, Massachusetts, area. The many open stitches include herringbone, buttonhole, and darning stitches. 1750–1800; H. 13 1/2" (41.91 cm); W. 67" (170.18 cm). The polychrome bottom panel, restyled in form, displays very delicate stitching with fine crewel yarns. New England; 1730–80; H. 8" (20.30 cm); W. 58 5/8" (148.90 cm).*

113

FIGURE 58

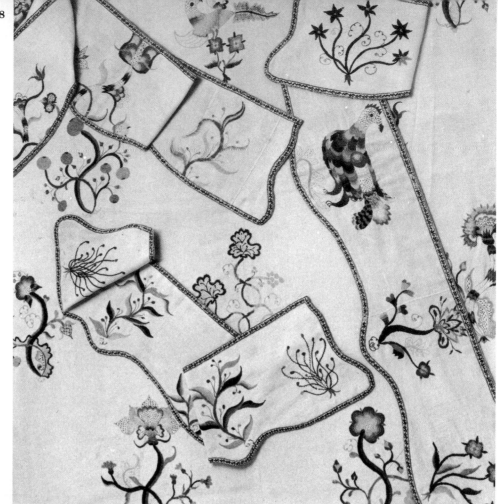

**Figure 58** *Three valances and a headcloth done by one embroiderer ( see also the bedspread in Plate 30). Bright crewel yarns in shades of red, blue, yellow, and green are worked in flat, bullion, buttonhole, chain, seed, whip, and darning stitches. Initials DAT [ ? ] in brown silk cross-stitch on the headcloth. The printed tape on the edges is a modern addition. Connecticut; 1740–80; H. (valances) 11 1/4" (28.57 cm); W. 56" (142.24 cm); H. 11 1/4" (28.57 cm); W. 79 1/2" (201.93 cm); H. (headcloth) 63 1/8" (161.29 cm); W. 63 1/8" (161.29 cm).*

**Plate 18** *This pocketbook, worked with silk yarns, is one of the finest known canvas-work examples. The embroiderer chose a superb color combination and artfully produced different textures with her choice of stitches. The blue green background is done in tent stitch that covers two squares with each stitch (on a 52-square-to-the-inch canvas). On the flowers, stems, or leaves, she covered only one square for each stitch, using the opposite angle as the background. The rougher texture in the rose and bell-like flower on the flap comes from the cross-stitch. Probably Philadelphia; 1740–90. Owned by the Chester County Historical Society.*

114

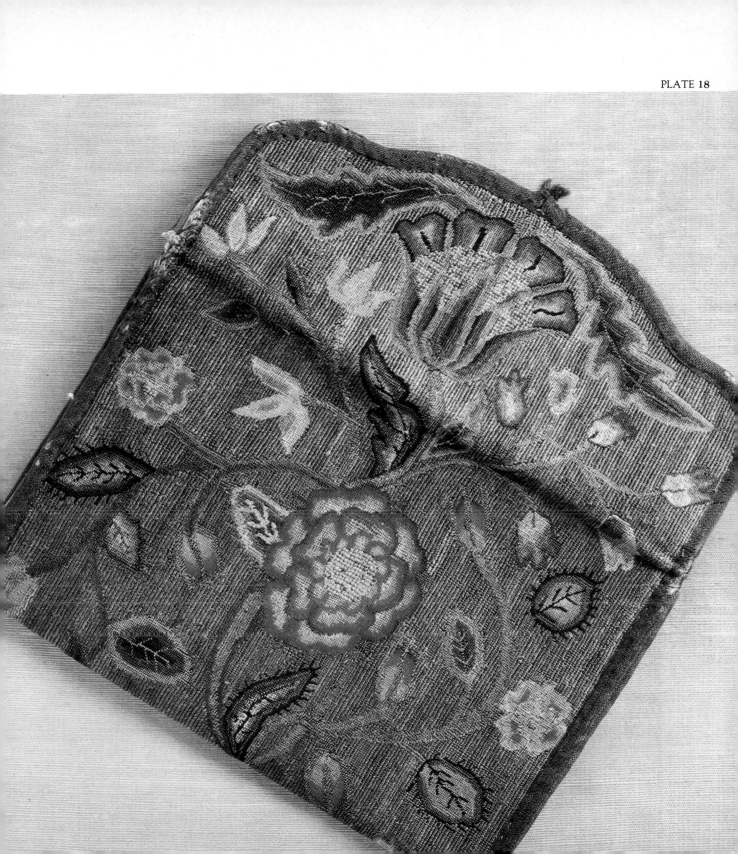

PLATE 18

PLATE 19

**Plate 19** *A useful item, a wall pocket done in the Irish stitch and dated 1766 by MH. The inside and back are not stitched or lined but are made of cardboard. Probably Pennsylvania; H. 10″ (25.40 cm); W. 8″ (20.32 cm).*

**Plate 20** *It is unusual in the twentieth century to obtain a group of works by one woman. These silk bags, purse, sewing cases, and pocketbooks were all worked by Mary Wright Alsop of Middletown, Connecticut. She ran the family shipping business after she was widowed. The Queen's-stitched pocketbook has her name, Mary Alsop x 1774. The other small Queen's-stitched pocketbook, with pink diamonds is unmarked. She knitted all the other pieces, in the early nineteenth century. The existing dates and initials indicate that they were presents to her children and their spouses.*

**Plate 21** *The inscription of this canvas work reads, "MARY OOTHOUT HER TABLE CLOATH SEPTEMBER THE ∗9∗1759." Pewter and delftware would have been fashionable tea items when this cloth first graced Mary's tea table. The rice stitch was used in the center area and for the lettering. Two of the carnations in the vase are worked in cross-stitch, the rest of the cloth in Irish stitch. H. 29 1/8″ (73.98 cm); W. 51 3/4″ (131.45 cm).*

PLATE 20

PLATE 21

PLATE 22

PLATE 23

to make these massive pieces of furniture as attractive as possible. Later, when the master bedroom was separated from the parlor, the bed retained its importance, as did bed hangings.

A well-appointed bed consisted of three valances (a fourth valance wasn't essential when the head of the bed stood against the wall, since the head cloth covered that upper area), the head cloth, two narrow side curtains near the head and two large side curtains, each wrapping around either side of the foot posts, a bedspread or coverlet, and bases attached to the bed rail. The lower edge and ends of the valances were shaped in various ways, according to the prevailing style of the day (Figure 58). Valances were unlined, finished only with a fine rolled hem and nailed to the framework of the bed.

Some families would hire an upholsterer to fit the master bed with hangings. These were made of fine fabrics and were usually trimmed with an elaborate tape or fringe. However, few of these survive today—further evidence that a family valued its homemade work over work done for it by professionals.

Even though bed hangings could indeed add to the impressiveness of a master bed, their function first and foremost was to keep the occupants warm. Only the very elderly or the wealthy afforded themselves the luxury of having a fire through the night, and since fireplaces lacked dampers, drafts whipped down into the room when no fire burned. In winter, the temperature inside a home could sink so low that "China cups cracked on the tea table . . . the instant the hot tea touched them," as Sarah Emery noted.[7] In very cold climates, eighteenth-century beds often bore heavy coverings called "rugs," which consisted of a sturdy background fabric, such as a heavy linen or woolen blanket, densely set with evenly raised loops of yarn (Plate 32; Figure 59). Woven bed rugs could also be purchased. (Rugs should not be confused with hooked rugs, which came later and were used on the floor. During the eighteenth century, floor coverings were called carpets.)

As the styles in bed furniture changed and hangings lost their popularity, the individual pieces of crewelwork were often used for other purposes. Few complete sets of hangings exist today, but the number of

**Plate 22** *An unfinished petticoat border in crewelwork. The inked design indicates the outlines and the areas for seed or darning stitches. A bewildered sheep stands on a hillock among strawberries as big as his head. Stitches are Roumanian couching, whip, French knots, seed, satin, and darning. Said to be from Litchfield, Connecticut; 1725–75; H. 7 1/4" (8.40 cm); W. 95" (241.30 cm).*

**Plate 23** *Fragment of a crewelwork panel, perhaps a petticoat border, with very fine yarns skillfully worked in Roumanian couching, whip, and seed stitches. H. 25 15/16" (65.70 cm); W. 7 7/16" (18.90 cm).*

FIGURE 59

FIGURE 61

FIGURE 60

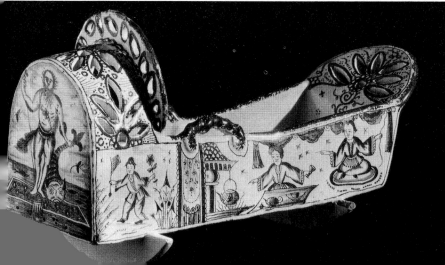

FIGURE 62

FIGURE 63 FIGURE 64

**Figure 59** *The initials W/RB and the date 1783 on this bed rug are enclosed in a tombstone-shaped frame. The foundation was a mended and patched old woolen blanket, worked in heavy wool yarn in the running stitch. The rhythmic design is worked in shades of blue, white, and dark brown. Probably Norwalk-New London area of Connecticut; H. 90″ (228.60 cm); W. 87″ (220.98 cm).*

**Figure 60** *A blue and white delftware cradle used in some areas as a container for small gifts such as pins or money for a new mother during her sitting-up visits. Dated 1736; initialed HT; decorated in Chinese taste; probably Holland.*

**Figure 61** *Delftware caudle or posset pot decorated in blue, orange red, green, and yellow. Caudle was so commonly served at christening parties and visits to the new mother that Webster's 1806 Compendious Dictionary called it "child-bed food." Family recipes varied, but the basics included oatmeal, water, lemon, wine, and spices such as nutmeg and mace. Dated 1709; probably Lambeth, England.*

**Figure 62** *A Taufschein, the baptismal certificate of a Pennsylvania German child. This one marks the birth on December 15, 1827, of Johannes Machemer, son of Jacob and Catharina Machemer of Turbot Township, Pennsylvania.*

**Figure 63** *Movable wooden toy—two pecking roosters. United States or Europe; 1800–60.*

**Figure 64** *Five movable wooden horses on a rectangular base. When the crank is turned, the horses seem to gallop. Europe or United States; 1800–75.*

FIGURE 6

individual pieces extant attest to their popularity.

There were numerous other bed linens for the mistress of a household to decorate. While pregnant, a woman would prepare her best sheets, which would be on display when relatives and friends came to visit her as a new mother. The cradle or basket linens were also of import, being carefully marked and perhaps trimmed with lace. Fine crib or christening blankets were made ready, both to keep an infant warm, and for show. In New England, new mothers often demonstrated their skills by embroidering a wool blanket with crewel yarns (Plate 31). An 1840 needlework book adopted from *The Spectator,* an early eighteenth-century English magazine popular in the colonies, the rather rigid stricture that "no one be actually married until she hath the child-bed pillow, &c., ready stitched, as likewise the mantle for the boy quite finished." [8]

This "mantle" was the baby's christening gown, which was often used for generations and sometimes became a family heirloom. In 1758, the inventory of John Turner of Sturbridge, Massachusetts, listed "To fine Little Baby things—10 shillings," probably a reference to the family's christening clothes. [9] Sarah Emery recalled a more common fate for a christening gown: "Grandmother Little owned a famously embroidered, linen cambric christening frock, and this garment having done service at all baptisms was now remodeled for my Sunday dress." [10]

Typical gifts for a newborn and the new mother included a silver coral and bells, a silver spoon, or a pincushion stuck with handmade pins in a pattern (Figures 60, 61, 62, 63, and 64). In some regions a pincushion hung on the front door to announce the birth (Figure 65).

Busy young mothers could practice their fancy needlework skills only in their spare moments, usually while supervising their bustling households. As the woman sat sewing, she could observe and direct both servants and children and still be productive herself. In this respect, fancy sewing served the same function for a woman of means as plain sewing did for the common housewife—it allowed her time to relax a little.

Relaxation was indeed at a premium in these days, not only in terms of time but also because of the corsets and stays that women of the better sort wore. Corsets rigidly molded the body into an inverted conelike form

**Figure 65** *A satin pincushion hung on doors in the New York region to announce the birth of a baby. Handmade pins spell out a revealing eighteenth-century phrase that suggests the distance parents maintained from their newborn children: "Welcome Little Stranger." America; dated 1770.*

WELCOME
LITTLE
STRANGER

1770

123

FIGURE 66

**Figure 66** *Corsets, stays (or busks), and one-piece, light blue silk petticoat, quilted in fine running stitches. This type of corset molded a woman's figure into a long-waisted, conical shape; America; 1750–85.*

**Figure 67** *A Pennsylvania German hand towel made by Mary Stamm in 1845 with very fine cross-stitches in red and pink linen thread. Her towel is pictured in the drawer of a Pennsylvania dower chest, the painted flowers of which also show characteristic Germanic designs. H. 51 1/4" (130.20 cm); W. 16 9/16" (42.10 cm).*

by pushing the bustline unnaturally high and molding the waistline very low. Usually the central placket contained a removable stay, called a busk, which was made of wood or ivory and left the wearer no choice but to practice the erect posture she had been taught in the day and boarding schools (Figure 66). Only when she was ill would a woman appear without the restricting garments. A tutor on the Carter plantation in Virginia, Philip Fithian found it so unusual when Mrs. Carter removed her stays one day that he recorded it in his diary. [11]

Unlike plain sewing, fancywork could not be done at night, since neither candles nor firelight produced sufficient light for this intricate stitchery. Even under the best conditions, the strain on the eyes that it caused usually forced a woman to give up fancy sewing by age forty-five

124

FIGURE 6

FIGURE 68

126

or fifty. Eyeglasses did not become common until late in the eighteenth century, and even then, they often weren't effective enough when it came to delicate work.

A woman was likely to be most productive as a needleworker in the few years between the time she left school and the time she married. During this period, free of responsibilities of running her own household, she had the time to make not only bed linens, towels, and other items for her dowry, but also accessory pieces, many for gifts (Figures 67 and 68). In the years just before her marriage in 1761, Elizabeth Drinker of Philadelphia completed a startling number of needlework items—ninety-three in all—each one of which she carefully recorded. Most of these pieces were small: "a round Pincushion" or ". . . a Queen Stitch cover for Polly's twezer case"; however, some were more substantial and more time-consuming, such as "a large Woosted Bible Cover" (Plate 33).[12]

A woman did not stop learning when she left her last sewing class as a schoolgirl. She could pick up a new stitch or the technique for a new effect from the women in whose company she sewed. Or, if she lived in one of the bigger cities, she could even attend a class to keep abreast of the latest styles. In her January 27, 1774, advertisement in *Rivington's New York Gazeteer,* Sarah Long of London mentioned the subjects she offered to teach young ladies and then added, "GROWN LADIES may be taught the TAMBOUR by lesson, as a room is set apart for that purpose. A compleat assortment of the very best Tambour silks for shadings are provided, with the best needles and cases and will be sold at the lowest prices." Obviously, sewing teachers offered in their advertisements an enticing array of needlework supplies, not just for their young pupils but also for the girls' mothers.

The prosperous women who lived in the prominent cities of Philadelphia, Boston, New York, and Charleston usually had the most time to pursue fancy needlework. Affluent enough to rely on the products and services of bakers, brewers, candlemakers, soap makers, fabric merchants, launderers, ironers, dry cleaners, and dressmakers, they had far less of a burden in caring for their homes and families. Moreover, they had their pick of indentured servants and slaves, who were more plentiful in these

**Figure 68** *An unknown woman, M. K created fantastic birds and animals in red and navy cross-stitches on this hand towel. The lower section is finished with knotting in a diamond pattern; Pennsylvania; 1800–70; H. 48 1/2" (123.20 cm); W. 13 1/16" (33.10 cm)*

large port cities. In contrast, women of the better sort in smaller towns, such as Newburyport, Annapolis, Deerfield, Saybrook, and Charlotte, had fewer conveniences and on the whole less time for fancy needlework.

The majority of these women, wherever they lived, functioned within the confines of their culture. It is important to understand the basic principles of their subordination, in order to appreciate the character of these women and the character they brought to their work. Legally they were the wards of their husbands. Any property or money a woman might have owned before her marriage or any that she earned during it automatically became her husband's sole possession to manage or dispose of as he pleased. Only rarely did a father have the will and foresight to arrange a prenuptial agreement for his daughter that mitigated these rigid laws.

Men "exercise nearly a perpetual guardianship over them [women], both in their virgin and their married state; and she who, having laid a husband in the grave, enjoys an independent fortune, is almost the only woman who among us can be called free." So wrote Englishman William Alexander in 1796 in his two-volume *The History of Women,* one of the earliest works on the subject. [13]

A married woman had no legal rights to her children, quite aside from the fact that by custom the father reigned as the final authority in the home. Alexander wrote, "A father only is empowered to exercise a rightful authority over his children, and no power is conferred on the mother." [14] If her husband died, a woman still could not expect to gain control of her children automatically. Another man was often appointed their guardian.

As late as 1848, the first Women's Rights Convention, held in Seneca Falls, New York, employed the classic term *civilly dead* to describe a married woman's legal position. [15] And if women were civilly dead inside the home, they were civil nonentities outside. Only men voted, and only they made laws and ordinances, including those that directly affected women. Women were completely excluded from the political arena, along with the many men who did not meet the restrictive voting requirements of early American society.

128

This legal subordination of women persisted until the twentieth century. Yet real situations often diverged from legal formality, particularly during the seventeenth century and most of the eighteenth. Although class-conscious, colonial society was on the whole rather open and it often ignored the restrictive laws against women, which it had inherited from the much more stratified Old World. This was a rapidly expanding culture of men set on improving their lot, and women proved to be rather handy, indeed necessary, accomplices. Men frequently ignored the legal niceties of keeping women in their places. Later, this unstructured, pioneer atmosphere gave way to a more stuffy propriety when economic growth entailed more sophisticated business arrangements than those of husbands and wives working side by side, as spouses often did in early colonial times.

Only toward the end of the eighteenth century did women lose access to their husbands' business affairs and experience the tightening of legal restrictions. Throughout the colonial years, however, many spouses had maintained a kind of practical equality in their marriages. Courts went so far as to favor the women who sued to act as their own agents after their husbands had deserted or otherwise shown themselves unable to support them. Because the members of colonial society viewed poverty as sinful, they preferred women who were financially independent, especially if the alternative was for them and their children to become public charges. However, since indigency was considered to be a grave social wrong, a girl's parents usually took care to entrust her only to a husband who had firmly established himself vocationally, thereby demonstrating that he could support a family.

We know that many women assisted their husbands vocationally, since many continued the family business after the man of the house died. To do this, a woman needed to be thoroughly familiar with her husband's trade, for she had to oversee an apprentice or hired journeyman who took over the actual work. Some women simply carried on by themselves, though not always without encountering resistance. Mary Roberts, the widow of a painter and engraver in Charleston, announced in the *South Carolina Gazette* of February 2–9, 1740, "Face Painting well performed by the said Mrs. Roberts. . . ." Apparently, the predominantly male clientele that had

FIGURE 69

patronized her husband needed further persuasion, and on September 12, 1743, she advertised, "It has been reported that the Subscriber cannot print Copies off Copper Plates &c. . . . this is to certify that the same is a manifest Falsehood, for that she is ready and willing to serve all Gentlemen and others as shall be pleased to employ her for that Purpose."

The clever, genteel Mrs. Samuel Provoost of New York became one of the most successful of these widows-turned-entrepreneurs. In order to attract customers to her counting house, located on a side street, she hit upon the idea of installing a sidewalk of flat stones in front of the shop and adjacent to it, along the street. Accustomed to rounded cobblestone streets, the pedestrians in the city greeted this innovation as a relief as well as a novelty, and Mrs. Provoost gained more business as well as the distinction of bringing the sidewalk to New York. She was so successful, both socially and financially, that the area of her shop became known as "Petticoat Lane," and when she remarried in 1721, she literally took in the business of her husband, enlarging the counting house to include space for his law practice. At the same time, she made elaborate legal arrangements permitting her to carry on her business and to ensure her financial independence. This remarkably successful career woman was also the mother of three children. [16]

Though always a minority, skilled business and professional women—single, married, and widowed—entered a wide range of fields: tavern keeping, paper hanging, dry goods and seed merchandising, upholstering, glass engraving, artistry in wax and miniatures, publishing, importing, midwifery and medicine, laundering, dentistry, brewing, even circus performing. Most frequently of all, working women earned their living at teaching and needlework, often both.

Even if they weren't needleworkers, these women who participated in fields outside of homemaking give us some insight into the lives of those who were. They show us that, while in the minority, it was possible for even a woman of some standing to combine the roles of housewife, mother, and at the same time a professional. They, like their poorer counterparts, did what needed doing, whether it was nursing a sick child or running the family business when the man of the house couldn't. Working outside the

**Figure 69** *All linen cut work, pointing, or needle lace sampler signed by Sarah Wayn [e], 1787. In spite of her proficiency in cut work, she did not leave enough space for her last name. Sarah Wayne was probably the daughter of the Philadelphia cabinetmaker William Wayne. H. 6 7/8" (17.48 cm); W. 7 1/8" (18.11 cm).*

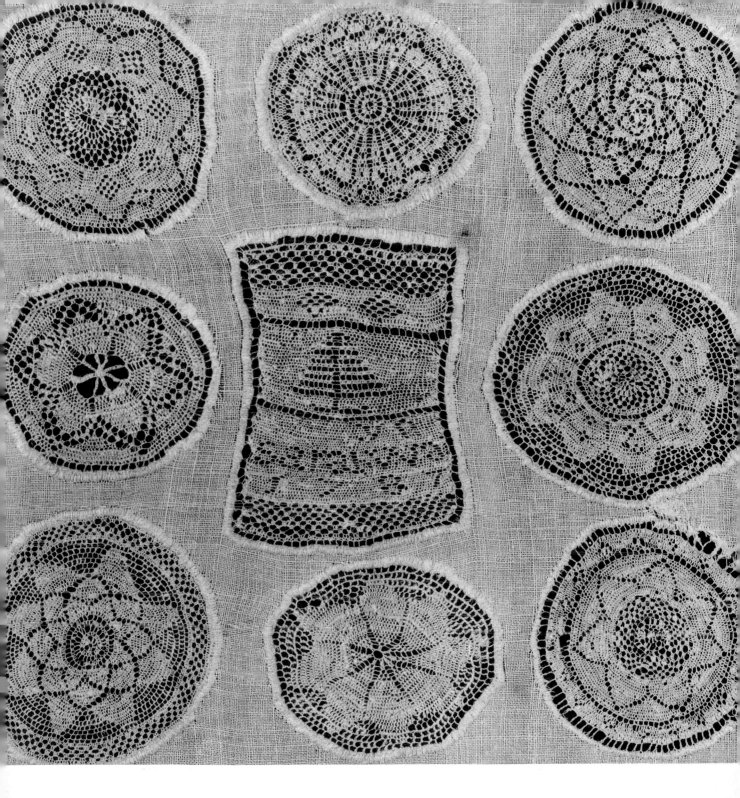

home did not relieve women of their regular household duties—it only added to them, leaving less opportunity or inclination for fancy diversions.

✿ ✿ ✿ ✿ ✿

Perhaps the most demanding form of fancywork that colonial women who had the time produced was lacework, a generic term that includes many delicate openwork techniques, all of them requiring great skill and patience. Although the finished product was expensive, and as such a symbol of those wealthy enough to wear it, the task of lace-making hardly pampered those who performed it.

During the years that social custom was dominated by the Puritans, there was social censure for any but those in the higher orders of society who wore lace. This behavior prevailed for about as long as it took those a bit lower in the social pecking order to be able to afford lace. During the seventeenth, eighteenth, and early nineteenth centuries, stylish men favored lavish amounts of lace gracing their shirt fronts and cuffs. Women used it for ornamenting dresses, aprons, handkerchiefs, and baby clothing. By the eighteenth century, the colonies were importing sizable quantities of lace from England, and in mid-century the better American sewing schools were teaching their girls how to make lace. Advertisements regularly offered all sorts of lacework supplies.

American needleworkers practiced four forms of lacework before the nineteenth century: cut work, Dresden work, netting, and bobbin lace.

The fine white work samplers (Figure 69), products of the day and boarding schools during the last half of the eighteenth century, best illustrate the technique of cut work. Because the work was so fragile, few examples of it remain. To do cut work, the needlewoman would enclose an area of linen background material with a securing stitch such as the satin or buttonhole stitch. She would then cut away the entire enclosed area and, in a very taxing and tedious process, fill in the empty space with variations of the buttonhole stitch. This technique was also known as pointing.

In Dresden work, instead of starting with a completely empty area, the needleworker systematically removed certain weft or warp threads from the background material in the design area. She then used embroidery

FIGURE 70

**Figure 70** *A hand towel by Elisaeet Rauch hanging on a door. In the upper section, flower trees were worked in cross-stitches of red and beige. The lower square is drawn work with stars and an angular plant embroidered in white cotton yarn. Pennsylvania; 1800–50; H. 64 3/4" (164.40 cm); W. 16 1/16" (40.70 cm).*

133

FIGURE 71

**Figure 71** *Small pocketbook in silk Queen's stitch, found containing a piece of sheer white cotton embroidery partially stitched to its inked paper pattern, visible through the fabric. The flowers were worked in satin stitch with handmade netted centers. America; 1790–1810; H. 3 1/2" (8.26 cm); W. 4 3/16" 10.64 cm).*

stitches to draw, or "weave," the remaining ground yarns together into lacelike designs. Needlework teachers who advertised instruction in Dresden work sometimes called it "weave lace" or the "Berlin needle work" (not to be confused with the later, Victorian canvas work called "Berlin work"). Pennsylvania hand towels (Figure 70) often show a coarser form of this technique.

Bobbin lace, also called bobbin, bobbinet, bone, blond, and, more recently, pillow lace, employed a number of slender bones, or bobbins, each of which was wound with thread. By knotting and interlocking the threads from the bobbins around pins, each inserted vertically into a strategic design point in a pattern laid over a specially made, rounded, firm pillow, the lace maker could create elaborate openwork patterns. Although early in the nineteenth century needlework instructors increasingly advertised bobbinet lace among the skills they taught, it was too complex an undertaking to gain great appeal as an accomplishment. Some women, especially in New England, earned their living producing it early in the nineteenth century.

Netting took its name from the background material used for it— not a plain-woven material such as fine muslin, but a fine mesh, either handmade or machine-made. The needleworker added her embroidery stitches in delicate designs to this netlike mesh. *Net work* also indicated the process of creating the background net. By using a variety of different stitches, a woman could produce interesting effects, such as those in the center of the flower shown in Figure 71. One of the few advertisements to offer instruction in all lacelike techniques was Elizabeth Wilson's in *The Pennsylvania Ledger and Weekly Advertiser* for May 20, 1775, "Dresden Work, Pointing, Bobbing, and Netting Lace."

Lacework was demanding and time-consuming. Then tambour work came to America. The first evidence of this new fancywork appeared in the late 1760s. A milliner, Mrs. Bontamps, announced in the *Philadelphia Gazette* for December 29, 1768, that she "embroiders in Gold, Silver, Silk and Thread, upon the late invented Tambour." Suddenly women without the skill or patience for lacework found to their delight that they could produce a similar effect (Figure 72). They used tambour work to create lacy-looking designs with silk, cotton, or crewel thread on the lightweight muslins or silks of dresses, scarves, window draperies, and bed hangings. Tambour was easy to learn, quickly done, and, as such, an instant hit.

Instead of a needle, the tambour worker used a hook with a narrow decorative handle and fitted with one of an assortment of various-sized, sharp, V-shaped hooks. First, the tambour worker inserted the hook down between threads of the fabric, which was stretched tautly over a frame (Figure 73). Then, while holding the top of the handle with one hand from above the frame, she used her other hand to loop the thread onto the hook below the fabric and frame. Next, she pulled the hook and the loop of thread back up through the material, leaving the small loop of thread resting on the material. Then she reinserted the hook just inside the first

**Figure 72** *Tambour-worked fragment in colored yarns; probably United States; 1790–1830; H. 8 1/8" (20.65 cm); W. 35 1/2" (90.17 cm). (Gift of Mrs. Francis White.)*

FIGURE 72

136

loop to bring up a second loop of thread. This second loop would surface inside the edge of the first and extend beyond it, so that the tension of the thread loops would hold their shapes. In this way the tambour worker began to create a chain of loops, each one anchoring the previous one to the background material.

Tambour work established itself rapidly. In January, 1772, for example, one wealthy gentleman from Philadelphia, John Cadwalader, bought a fine wooden tambour frame for his wife, Elizabeth, from the prominent cabinetmaker Thomas Affleck for the considerable sum of two pounds.[17] During the 1770s, numerous newspaper advertisements appeared from teachers offering instruction in tambour work (to adult women as well as their daughters). In addition, merchants advertised their lines of tambour work supplies. One such announcement, from *Rivington's New York Gazeteer* of July 17, 1774, heralded "A compleat assortment of TAMBOUR SHADES on SILK and SHANEIL, with the best London made Tambour needles, and cases." Various merchants in the colonies also imported finished pieces of tambour work.

The popularity of handmade tambour work lasted for some fifty years. Then in 1834, a Paris exhibition unveiled a machine with which a single operator could produce tambour stitches at one hundred and forty times the rate of a woman working by hand. Tambour work died as quickly as it had arisen, and today fine handmade projects are virtually nonexistent.

The popularity of tambour work, short-lived though it proved to be, foreshadowed the beginning of a new era in American needlework, and in the life-styles of fancy needleworkers. The number of affluent women in the colonies was growing, and as these women increased in number, they also gradually grew less isolated in their homes. Affluent women became more gregarious and sophisticated, with less time for the most demanding and intricate needlework forms. Tambour work brought them the rewards of fancy needlework without requiring quite so much effort and concentration. In short, fancy needlework, like life in general, was becoming a bit easier.

Interestingly, and naturally enough, as mothers indulged themselves more, they began to indulge their children more, too (Figures 74

**Figure 73** *Detail of all-white tambour work on muslin, and a tambour hook; probably United States; 1800–40.*

**Figure 74** *Child's banister-back chair supports a cloth doll that wears a brown chintz dress with rose and white flowers and a plaid apron. The small crewel-embroidered bag has many worn areas, exposing the brown inked design. The embroidery is crudely executed (possibly by a young child) in whip, satin, and seed stitches.*

FIGURE 74

and 75). By the beginning of the eighteenth century, the enlightened advisors on child-rearing began to recommend more lenient discipline for children when they were disobedient.

> . . . when Encouragement will do no good, Correction
> becomes Seasonable; when all fair Means and Perswasions
> prevail not, there is a necessity of using sharper; let that be
> first try'd in words. I mean not by railing and foul Language,
> but in a sober yet sharp Reproof. And if that fail too, then
> proceed to Blows. . . . the Power of Parents over their
> Children . . . should be exercised with Equity and
> Moderation. [18]

Here was quite a departure from the standard procedure of humiliations and whippings as a first resort. Diaries reveal that even such cultured

FIGURE 75

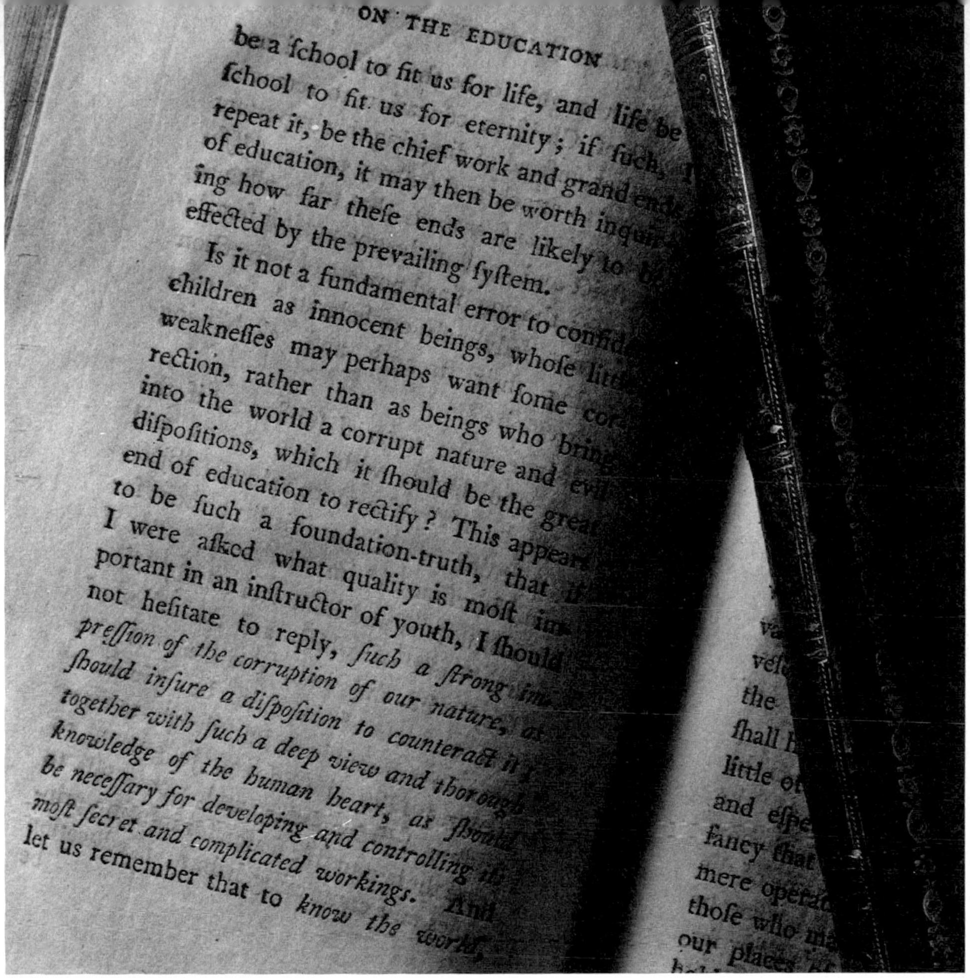
ON THE EDUCATION
be a ſchool to fit us for life, and life be
ſchool to fit us for eternity; if ſuch,
repeat it, be the chief work and grand end
of education, it may then be worth inqu
ing how far theſe ends are likely to
effected by the prevailing ſyſtem.
Is it not a fundamental error to conſid
children as innocent beings, whoſe litt
weakneſſes may perhaps want ſome cor
rection, rather than as beings who brin
into the world a corrupt nature and evi
diſpoſitions, which it ſhould be the grea
end of education to rectify? This appear
to be ſuch a foundation-truth, that
I were aſked what quality is moſt im
portant in an inſtructor of youth, I ſhould
not heſitate to reply, *ſuch a ſtrong im-*
*preſſion of the corruption of our nature,* as
*ſhould inſure a diſpoſition to counteract* it
*together with ſuch a deep view and thorough*
*knowledge of the human heart, as ſhould*
*be neceſſary for developing and controlling*
*moſt ſecret and complicated workings.* And
let us remember that to *know the world,*

FIGURE 76

**Figure 75** *Specially made child's toy cup, saucer, tea caddy, teapot, and teapot stand of Chinese export porcelain with overglazed decoration picturing a boy and girl playing. Shown with a normal-sized tea caddy with an overglazed shield motif. China; 1800–10.*

**Figure 76** *Detail of Hannah More's influential two-volume* Strictures on the Modern System of Female Education, *vol. 1, p. 64. In this passage she sounded her disapproval of the long-held belief that children were born corrupt in nature.* DMMC, WM, LC1421/M.83.

men as William Byrd of Virginia and Samuel Sewall of Massachusetts frequently countenanced such severe punishments in their households.

It took some time for the modified view to gain support, but by 1804, the thoroughly respectable Englishwoman Hannah More was preaching in her *Strictures on the Modern System* that children's "little weakness may perhaps want some correction," but that children are not "beings who bring into the world a corrupt nature and evil disposition" (Figure 76).[19] The doctrine of original sin, which had ruled—or at least rationalized—the governing of children (and everyone else) for so long, had begun to lose its power. Soberness was no longer the prevailing theme for one's behavior, and enjoyment was more acceptable for all. Fancy needlework was soon to reflect this more leisurely view.

PLATE 26

PLATE 25

**Plate 24** *Crewelwork bedspread displaying exceptionally graceful and well-executed designs. The stitches are Roumanian couching, flat, herringbone, whip, satin, French knots, darning, and bullion. Embroidered at the top in the center in pink silk is A.L. to B.S./1774; probably Massachusetts; H.108 3/4" (278.02 cm); W.87 1/4" (224.28 cm).*

**Plate 25** *An unusual crewel-embroidered picture from Chester County by Elizabeth Taylor dated 1785. Several other crewelwork pictures with this same design are known, but they were done by different girls and signed with different dates. H.11 1/2" (29.21 cm); W. 9 3/4" (24.76 cm).*

**Plate 26** *This crewelwork headcloth with a tree of life is almost identical in design to one owned by Historic Deerfield, Inc. Notice the similarity in design to the printed Indian tree of life in Figure 113. Some of the linen background has been replaced. Stitches are Roumanian couching and whip. America; 1725–75; H. 74" (197.96 cm); W. 62 1/2" (158.75 cm).*

143

PLATE 24

PLATE 27

PLATE 29

PLATE 30

PLATE 28

144

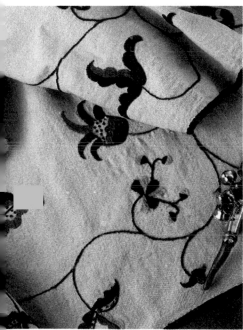

PLATE 31

**Plate 27** *Child's woolen petticoat with crewelwork decoration. Stitches are flat, whip, and cross. New England; 1740–80; H. 22 5/8" (57.47 cm).*

**Plate 28** *Solidly worked crewelwork slip seat, predominantly Roumanian couching with some whip and satin stitches. The woman's face is done in a silk darning stitch and probably once had small black beads for her eyes, as the cow, dog, and leopard still do. Probably Massachusetts; 1750–80; H. 15 1/4" (39.74 cm); W. 19 3/4" (59.15 cm). The pocket on the chair is worked in Roumanian couching, seed, fern, and buttonhole stitches. The initials E [? ]L are embroidered at the bottom of the slit. Probably Massachusetts; 1735–85; H. 15" (38.10 cm); W. 11 1/4" (28.58 cm).*

**Plate 29** *A happy, comical crewelwork panel. Birds as large as people compete for the ripe cherries and pears while various animals and more birds romp among the flowering vines on the hills. Silk yarn was used for many accents. Stitches are Roumanian couching, whip, seed, French knots, and satin. This unfinished panel is attributed to Mary Dodge Burnham of Newburyport, Massachusetts. 1725–60; H. 16 1/4" (41.30 cm); W. 61 7/8" (157.20 cm).*

**Plate 30** *Vigorous design on a crewelwork bedspread from Connecticut, probably by the same embroiderer as the valances in Figure 58. Shown here with other crewelwork hangings. Stitches are Roumanian couching, bullion, flat, buttonhole, seed, whip, herringbone, weaving, and chain. Bedspread 1740–80; H. 93 1/4" (236.86 cm); W. 111 1/2" (283.21 cm).*

**Plate 31** *Small woolen crewelwork blanket probably for a crib; the stitches are done in Roumanian couching, whip, and cross. New England; 1760–1800; H. 33" (83.82 cm); W. 43 1/4" (109.86 cm). A pink silk satin cushion on which various sized pins form the design; a silver coral and bells with a whistle at one end.*

145

PLATE 32

PLATE 33

**Plate 32** *Mary Foot[e], who lived in Colchester, Connecticut, created this darned bed rug, presumably for her marriage in 1778 to Nathaniel Otis. Mary started with a plain woven woolen ground and sewed her design in large, blue darning stitches, pulling each stitch level and rather taut; she did not leave raised loops, customarily found in bed rugs. She completely covered the white background in an even-textured darning pattern. Mary's sister Elizabeth made a very similar rug, now owned by the Connecticut Historical Society. A third one, probably by her sister Abigail, is at Historic Deerfield, Inc. H. 83 1/2" (212.09 cm); W. 77 1/2" (196.85 cm).*

**Plate 33** *Finely worked Irish-stitched canvas cover for a Bible, done with crewel yarns and white silk to outline the design. The embroiderer carefully planned her design so that she used a different pattern for the part of the covering that went over the spine. There are forty stitches to the inch. Written on one of the pages in this Bible, which was printed in London in 1685, is "Phobe Guest [?] her Bible given her by her mother ye 15 day of ye 10 month 1691." Another entry indicates that Phobe gave it to her daughter Debbe Morris in 1738. The cover was probably worked by Debbe Morris. Philadelphia area; 1730–70. Owned by the Chester County Historical Society.*

FIGURE 77

# **4** Diversions for Genteel Ladies
## *The Age of Accomplishments*

For women the end of the eighteenth century and the beginning of the nineteenth was an exhilarating time. This was especially true for the women with sufficient wealth to keep up with the evolving styles. They could—indeed were almost expected to—do more than sit home and manage their households. Many new intellectual outlets and possibilities for socializing beckoned. Much of this new social life was frivolous, but it held a new and serious idea about the proper role of women and fostered the growth of the new outlook. "In the present state of society," a prominent male Philadelphian wrote in 1810, "woman is inseparably connected with everything that civilizes, refines, and sublimates man."[1]

The observer, Joseph Hopkinson, was writing as a friend of the fine arts, complimenting women for their interest in advancing cultural ideals. But his words might just as easily have served as the rationale for all the other forms of social activity in which women of the better sort participated during this period. In an age in which wealthy Americans strived to be genteel, women were considered most capable of appreciating, indeed nurturing, gentility.

In 1784, Nancy Shippen Livingston, a twenty-one-year-old woman living with her parents after she had separated from her husband, recorded how she thought a lady of her station should spend each day. Since she was not the mistress of a household—so that what she did with her leisure time resembled more a single girl's pastimes than a married woman's—the daily schedule she proposed no doubt overemphasized the new priorities of the fancy ladies of the day. Nevertheless, her recommendations are intriguing. She allotted two hours a day for household management and five hours for accomplishments such as sewing and drawing—in which she included the instruction and observation of servants as they did household chores. Then she added three hours for meals—heavily laden with conversation—and five more hours for socializing. [2]

Five hours a day of socializing! To fill such a schedule required more than incidental contact with a few friends. Starting in the last quarter of the eighteenth century, women of Nancy Livingston's social class engaged in an elaborate round of visiting and receiving visits. In diaries kept at this time by fashionable ladies, there is hardly a day's entry that does not

**Figure 77** *Catherine Butler probably made this mourning picture to commemorate her late brother. Because an 1806 Hartford, Connecticut, newspaper was glued to the back, it is likely that Catherine lived in this vicinity and attended a local school. A group of pictures like this one, with the apparel appliquéd in separate fabrics, sheer black crepe on the adults and white on the baby, came from this region of Connecticut. Rows of chenille yarns in the foreground complement the narrow strip of blue velvet appliquéd in the lower left. French knots, fern, and seed stitches accompany the solid areas of whipstitches. The faces and arms are painted. The linen edging, which originally held the picture to the needlework frame while it was being embroidered, is still on the piece.*

mention one or two visits.

Some visits were made to acknowledge a special occasion. For example, two or three weeks after a woman had given birth, she entertained her acquaintances at a "sitting up visit," at which callers could admire the good health of the baby and leave presents (Plate 34).

A marriage merited a "bride's visit," in some areas as soon as a day after the ceremony but as long as a month afterward in others. In 1786, Hannah Thomson, wife of a Philadelphia government official, noted that in New York the husband as well as the bride received congratulatory callers: "The Gentlemans Parents keep open house just in the same manner as the Brides Parents. The Gentlemen go from the Bridegroom house to drink Punch with and to give joy to his Father. The Brides Visitors go In the same manner from the Brides to his Mothers to pay their compliments to her."[3]

Such special events as births and marriages occurred too infrequently to satiate the desire for socializing that the newly gregarious ladies of the day possessed. Instead of waiting for special occasions, these women made visiting an integral part of their daily routine. Sarah Emery noted that in her town, Newbury, Massachusetts, outside Boston, "fashionable ladies devoted the morning to calling or receiving visitors. . . . There was little ceremonious visiting of an afternoon, unless invitations had been issued for a tea party" (Figure 78).[4] However, in most regions, visiting was customarily done in the afternoon.

At their get-togethers, women might snack on cake and wine or play cards, all the while having some relatively undemanding kind of fancy needlework, such as tambour or knitting, nearby. Above all, of course, they talked. Since the tempo of an afternoon was bound to lag without it, good conversation became an essential ingredient for a successful visit, whatever the other diversions. When Rebecca Franks, a Philadelphian, visited New York City in 1781, she wrote home to her sister in disgust, ". . . few New York ladies know how to entertain company in their houses unless they introduce the card tables . . . I don't know a woman or girl that can chat above half an hour, and that on the form of a cap, the colour of a ribbon or the set of a hoop-stay" (Figure 80).[5]

FIGURE 78

**Figure 78** *Tea table set with molded English salt-glazed stoneware. A crewelwork potholder on a diaper ground. Stitches are seed, chain, whip, and Roumanian couching in shades of blue green, yellow, and brown. When a silver spoon was laid across a tea cup, it signified the guest wanted no more tea. Potholder: America; 1750–1800; H. 7 5/8" (19.38 cm); W. 6 7/8" (17.48 cm).*

In addition to daytime visiting, there were dinner parties and balls to attend at night. Sarah Emery noted in her reminiscences:

> *Dinner parties were common, when the table would be loaded with luxuries. After dessert the ladies retired to the parlor for an hour's gossip, while the gentlemen sipped wine, smoked long Dutch pipes, and discussed the affairs of the nation. The ladies having been rejoined in the drawing room, coffee was passed.*

She recalled that dances were held in a specially built hall, considered excellent for dancing because it had a spring floor. While the young courting couples danced, their parents played cards in anterooms. [6]

This increased socializing on the part of women did not alter the fact that certain basic factors in their lives had not changed. The Declaration of Independence and most of the subsequent enlightened writings pertained exclusively to the rights of white males. Women's subordinate legal role remained. While historians disagree on the effects of the post–Revolutionary War period on women, there is no denying that it was a transitional period for them. Some historians believe that this era marked the end of an economic partnership between women and their mates, which resulted in a loss of stature. Other historians claim that the expanding economy and the Industrial Revolution offered women not only more leisure time, but—at least briefly—varying degrees of benefits from the enlightened ideas.[7] Without question, women's scholastic opportunities improved owing to the enlightenment, even though the seminaries continued to stress an ever-widening group of accomplishments. Painting on velvet, singing, piano playing, water colors, and hair work vied with the new needlework forms for the fashionable young woman's attention.

In dating the various needlework fads of this period, the extraordinarily well-kept records of the Moravians are most informative, since the Moravians taught most of these accomplishments at their school in Bethlehem, Pennsylvania. References to glass beads, for example, begin to appear in the Moravian accounts of the 1790s. To have a "Glass Pocket Book" made up cost "Cath. Boudinot 1 £, 6s, on June 17, 1797." Glass beads were also used to decorate pincushions, needle holders, and bags.

Beginning in 1819, one of the sisters at the Moravian school specialized in ribbon work, a technique in which one gathered and tacked down a ribbon, using specially dyed ribbon in graduated shades of one color. The finished trim could be used on a dress or simply as an ornament in itself for framing. By 1826, the students at the Moravian school were apparently using strips of silk crepe in addition to ribbon for this sort of work.[8] A girl could fold and gather these strips of crepe to simulate a bouquet of flowers, for example. Such a design could project an inch or more from the background and thus required a very deep frame, usually one without glass. Crepe-work creations were great dust-catchers.

Painting on velvet, yet another accomplishment, enjoyed a vogue in New England and the middle states during the first third of the nineteenth century. The girls and women who did this work favored simple fruit-and-flower scenes or mourning themes (Figure 79).

Women did Marseilles quilting to make their petticoats showy. Because many stylish dresses before 1800 were fashioned with an open panel in front from the waist to the hem, the front of the petticoat was beautifully displayed. Like tambour work, Marseilles quilting was a holdover from the pre-Revolutionary period. Advertisements dating as early as 1749 mentioned this technique.

The term *Marseilles quilting* was actually a misnomer, since by definition quilting binds together three layers of fabric, and in this technique, only two are joined, with artistically shaped areas of filling between them. The finished product resembled those done with the techniques that are known today as stuffed work and corded work. To work a piece of Marseilles quilting, the needlewoman would pick a loosely woven cotton

**Figure 79** *Many schools taught painting on velvet to young girls during the second quarter of the nineteenth century. Here the craft was applied to the Hamilton family arms, though coats-of-arms were unusual subjects for velvet painting. On this example, an 1813 newspaper was glued to its stretcher.*

**Figure 80** *A New York Chippendale card table and chair with its original Irish-stitched chair seat in shades of beige, pink, blue, and ivory. This one is part of a larger set of chairs, all with seats worked by Elizabeth Banker before her marriage in 1779. H. 16 1/4" (41.27 cm); W. 20 3/8" (51.76 cm). On the table the solidly worked crewelwork pocketbook, in shades of pink, orange, yellow, and green, probably shows the work advertised in the March 9, 1775, Boston News-Letter by Ruth Hern as "flowering with crewel-working Pocket-Books." The primary stitches are Roumanian couching; there are also touches of whip and herringbone. America; 1740–90; H. 3 7/8" (9.84 cm); W. 7 1/8" (18.10 cm).*

FIGURE 79

FIGURE **80**

PLATE 34

PLATE 35

PLATE 36

or linen to use for a backing fabric and a satin or fine plain-woven fabric for the front—one whose highlights would be best set off by the contours of the filling to come. She would then apply a design to the underside of the backing fabric, outlining the shape of every area to be filled. Next she stitched the two fabrics together along the design lines (Figure 82), using fine running or backstitches. Finally, she would use a sharp instrument to spread apart several yarns and insert cotton batting between them into each outlined area to create padded design areas. To pad flower stems or other narrow channels in the design, she would thread a large-eyed needle or bodkin with candlewick yarn and run it between the parallel lines of stitching (Figure 81).

Beginning about 1760, notices began to appear advertising imported, machine-made Marseilles quilting—for example, "Loom quilting for Petticoats" (*South Carolina Gazette*, May 21, 1772). Elizabeth Drinker mentions purchasing this type of product on May 4, 1778, when she "went out again after dinner to Shops, [and] bought merceals [sic] Quilting for Petticoats for the Girls."[9]

Despite industrial competition, women continued to practice hand-made Marseilles quilting until the 1830s, though after 1800 not for petticoats, since open-front dresses had gone out of style. Instead of petticoats, women used Marseilles quilting when making bed hangings and dressing table covers (Figure 83) for their households. After the 1830s, cheaper, more durable, factory-made "Marseilles spreads" doomed the handmade products. This machine-made product remained popular for so long (well into the twentieth century) that women of more recent times often forgot or never knew that Marseilles quilting had once been a hand-embroidery technique.

Candlewicking, like Marseilles quilting, was made by both hand and machine methods but later (starting about 1840) only by machine. For it, the needleworker used a rather heavy, porous cotton ground and embroidered it with soft, bulky yarns that resembled candlewicks; hence the name of the yarn and the technique (Figure 85). Sometimes women limited themselves to one or two stitches, usually French knots and the whipstitch, and produced a rather formal pattern (Figure 86). On other

**Plate 34** *Baby items: a pewter nursing bottle, a crocheted ball/rattle, a stuffed cloth rooster, a wooden ox pull-toy, and a Pennsylvania German birth and baptismal certificate (Taufschein).*

**Plate 35** *A hatchment with the banner bearing a young woman's name, 1758/JANE BROWN/AET. 15. The arms are of those of Browne of Weald Hall in Essex, England. It was worked in tent stitch on canvas, plus satin stitch on the mantling. It was somewhat unusual for a woman to do her own hatchment, and this may have been the work of a schoolgirl. Possibly Massachusetts. H. 31 1/2" (80.01 cm); W. 31 1/2" (80.01 cm).*

**Plate 36** *A spritely picture, probably intended as a mourning picture, by Lucy Nye, who noted that she was born April 4, 1799. Lucy apparently had no one to mourn, so instead of a name on the tomb she substituted a cheerful verse on paper: "Blossoms fruit/and flowers/together rise/and the whole/year in gay/ confusion lies." Stitches are whip and satin; face and arm are painted. Paper inserts are glued on the tomb and at the bottom. United States; 1810–20; H. 11 1/4" (29.58 cm); W. 10 7/8" (27.53 cm).*

FIGURE 81

**Figure 81** *Detail of stuffed and corded work, sometimes called Marseilles work. The left side shows the finer, upper layer of fabric in a raised pomegranate design. The right side illustrates the coarser under fabric, with heavy yarn corded through the narrow channels to simulate narrow vines. Worked by Mary Remington of East Greenwich, Rhode Island, in 1815. (See Plate 4 for her sampler.)*

**Figure 82** *Hand-drawn paper pattern for stuffed work. Grapes and pineapples were favorite motifs because the small segments could be filled and puffed up attractively. DMMC, WM, 75x132.*

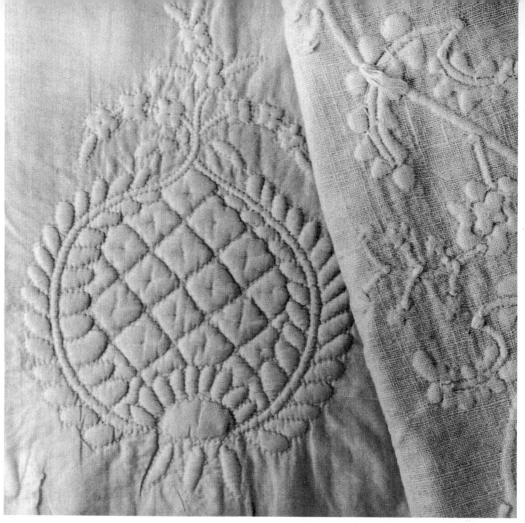

FIGURE 82

158

pieces, they used many different stitches, changed the thicknesses of the yarns, and with all this variety, created more exuberant designs (Figure 87).

A glance at the back of a piece of candlewick quickly reveals whether it was made by machine or by hand. If machine-made, it is smooth, neat, and even; if handmade, it is likely to be messy, a hodgepodge of knots, loops, and stretched yarns. Machine-made candlewick, with designs much like the old handmade work, remains popular today.

In addition to all these different needlework forms and the other non-needlework accomplishments, many fine sewing accessories were produced during this period. There were beautiful sewing boxes, whalebone yarn winders, enameled needle holders, ivory thimble cases, and inlaid and veneered wood worktables (Figures 88, 89, 90, and 91). These tables were among the first pieces of fine furniture made specifically for women. To be sure, women had always had such essential work accessories as spinning wheels, yarn winders, looms, and embroidery frames (Figure 92). But the selection of fine furniture had been a man's province. Now, in a more affluent society, with its new regard for feminine refinement, women gained their own fine furniture, intended for both practical use and display. Early sewing tables, for example, came with a decorative cloth or wooden bag that served as a holder for needlework supplies. Later, Empire-styled tables had fittings that served as book rests or opened out to provide a small writing desk. Such a table was assuredly the prized display piece for a hostess welcoming guests to her parlor (Figure 93).

Through the mid-eighteenth century, needleworkers had made do with little more than pins, scissors, needles, and thread. By the nineteenth century, the stylish trappings of the craft were becoming almost as important as the needlework itself. Fancy needlework and its accessories became ornaments for the fashionable lady.

Even with these lovely needlework props and accessories, the early nineteenth century saw a definite decline in the quality of needlework. The pride in meticulous craftsmanship in both women's needlework and many men's crafts began to lose its importance. Apprenticeships for both men and women shortened and finally disappeared. At the same time,

FIGURE **83**

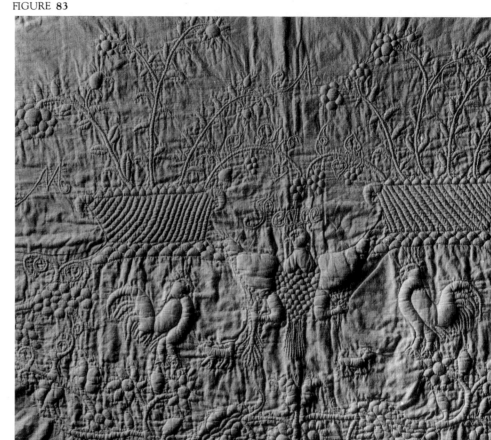

**Figure 83** *Half-oval dressing table cover of fine white cotton; Peace is stitched in script letters over the central eagle. The eagle is flanked by roosters and dogs. The initials MAW are said to be those of a member of the Westervelt family of New York. 1800–30; H. 23 3/4" (60.30 cm); W. 34 1/2" (87.60 cm).*

**Figure 84** *Not considered true candlewicking, this coverlet uses candlewicking materials but in a flatter, embroidered design. Stitches are feather, buttonhole, seed, whip, bullion, chain, French knots, Roumanian couching, and satin. United States; 1800–30; H. 110 1/2" (280.67 cm); W. 118 1/4" (300.35 cm).*

young girls spent fewer hours on fancy needlework training. Grown women no longer had the time or patience to create such ambitious, involved projects as canvas-work chair seats or upholstery. Now ladies of style preferred fancywork projects that were less involved and more portable, as well as showier. Needlework continued to have prestige as a feminine accomplishment, though now as a mark of gentility, not mere craftsmanship, in the rising cultural consciousness of the times.

A notice in the *Pennsylvania Gazette* for February 17, 1813, announcing the Third Annual Exhibition of the newly formed Pennsylvania Academy of Fine Arts, read, "In the last exhibition there were several

FIGURE **84**

productions (the work of female artists) consisting of original drawings, models in wax, pieces of needlework, &c., which were pronounced, by the best judges, equal to anything of the kind executed in Europe" (Plate 38).

Women of the previous generation would not have thought of publicly exhibiting their fancy needlework. There had been honor enough in using it to ornament the furnishings of the home. However, now fancy needlework acquired a totally new function—as handiwork that served to display a fashionable lady's genteel sensibilities. In some circles, a woman who did fine needlework ceased to be a craftsman and became an artist, and a woman who appreciated such work could consider herself a patron of the arts.

In 1810, after the Pennsylvania Academy's First Annual Exhibition, Joseph Hopkinson rhapsodized in the *Port Folio*, "Our collection of painting and statuary, from the first exhibition, has been visited by our ladies, with a constancy which acquits them of the motive of mere curiosity, and an ardour which could be found only in minds well improved, touched with the fire of genius, and really capable of enjoying her works." For Mr. Hopkinson, "the fire of genius" that sparked a woman to paint, draw, or do fancy needlework went hand in hand with "minds well improved." It was in this context that he made his remark about women being "inseparably connected with everything that civilizes, refines, and sublimates man." He didn't define "everything," but clearly he meant to include women's artistic, intellectual, and aesthetic sensibilities.[10]

**Figure 85** *Candlewick bedspread on a huckaback weave, boldly initialed H.J. Predominantly French knots with chain, whip, satin, and interwoven running stitches. United States; 1800–30; H. 98" (248.92 cm); W. 98" (248.92 cm).*

FIGURE **85**

As one facet of their personality, women of the better sort during these years were allowed to be lavishly self-indulgent, luxuriating in all the feminine high fashions and diverting entertainments of the day. They wore elegant clothing, played cards, went dancing, attended dinner parties and the theater, witnessed tight-rope performances and equitation acts, and, above all, visited, spending hours each day simply chatting with each other. Many men encouraged them in this luxurious leisurely life-style, probably because when one's wife had time to spend in this way, it signified a man's success.

Yet at the same time the idea of gentility required some intellectual as well as social refinement; a fashionable lady could no longer afford to be ignorant. The same boarding schools that were training their young ladies in the latest stylish accomplishments were also teaching them an expanded range of scholastic subjects. Women attended lectures on philosophy and ethics, visited the new natural history and art museums, wrote poetry, and published articles and books. Some women in a few of the large cities went so far as to hold a very modest form of a salon, where men and women discussed the new ideas as well as the new fashions of the day. The Age of Enlightenment was not confined to men, and genteel women as well as men were expected to cultivate their minds.

A few women of the period achieved renown for their worldly activities. Sarah Apthrop Morton, an active Bostonian who sponsored salon groups, published poetry, articles, and books under her pen name "Philenia." With her husband, Perez, she crusaded for repeal of the Boston law banning theater performances (Plate 37), and in 1791, seventeen years before the government passed a law outlawing the slave trade with Africa, she pleaded for an end to the trade. In the preface to *The Ruling Passion* by Thomas Paine, published in 1797, she was praised as "the American Sappho".[11]

The new style of female sophistication and women's widening horizons were reflected dramatically in women's fashions at this time. The last decade of the eighteenth century brought to America, as it did to Europe, a vogue for classicism. Roman motifs symbolized the new republican form of government. About 1800, women adopted the classical style in their dress, thereby initiating one of the most radical changes in fashion history.

In 1837, *The Young Lady's Friend* reviewed the fashion revolution this way: ". . . the ladies who had been encased in whalebone, buckram, and [an] abundance of quilted petticoats, stepped forth as Grecian goddesses, without any corsets, any petticoats, any fulness to their garments, or any heels to their shoes. White muslin dresses of the scantiest dimensions [were] drawn closely round the figure, with the shortest possible waists."[12]

After centuries of covering themselves with layers upon layers of clothes and rigid stays, young fashionable women and even most of the mature ones adopted this slim, high-waisted silhouette. Prominent women, such as Dolley Madison, wore this style, although their garments were usually made of less-revealing fabric than the younger women daringly wore. A gentleman who attended the wedding of Betsy Patterson and Jerome Bonaparte on Christmas Eve, 1803, remarked, "All the clothes worn by the bride might have been put in my pocket. . . . Beneath her dress she wore but a single garment."[13]

That would have been a chemise, a woman's sole concession to underwear and hardly enough to keep the libertines at bay. John Fanning Watson tittered that the clothes were "so thin and transparent . . . especially when between the beholder and a declining sun, as to make a modest eye sometimes instinctively avert its gaze."[14]

The conservatives were scandalized, of course. Hannah More gasped at "the unchaste costume, the unpure style of dress, and the indelicate statue-like exhibition of the female figure, [with] its seemingly wet and adhesive drapery."[15] Her description of "wet and adhesive drapery" sounds extreme, but a few women would actually immerse their clothing in water to accentuate the clinginess of the classical drapery. No doubt a few of the women who adopted this racy new costume secretly enjoyed provoking the cries of outrage. Better educated, more sophisticated, encouraged to express themselves, women were testing their new freedom, often defiantly. A few of them began to take on the previously unassailable topic of male superiority—even in print.

One woman, writing in the September, 1787 issue of the *Columbian Magazine*, confessed that she thought women generally could employ their

FIGURE 86

**Figure 86** *Candlewicking technique used for a formal design of French knots combined with whipstitch accents, all worked on a very fine white cotton background. Deep netted fringe. Probably New York; 1800–25; H. 88 3/4" (225.50 cm); W. 94" (246.38 cm).*

time better than in "scribbling," but she said that she felt compelled nevertheless to "lay down the needle and take up the pen." She wrote in reply to an article in Mathew Carey's *American Museum* that had twitted women for the way in which they whitewashed the interior of their homes. The male writer had noted that the bustle with which women pursued this housekeeping chore inevitably produced a wreckage of "halves of China bowls, cracked tumblers, broken wine glasses, tops of tea pots and stoppers of departed decanters." In refutation, this woman recounted her experience with her husband:

> *"He comes into the parlour the other day, where, to be sure,*
> *I was cutting up a piece of linen. Lord, says he, what a clutter*

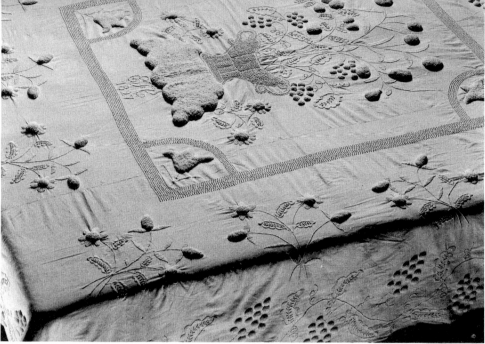

FIGURE 87

**Figure 87** *Exceptionally high tufting on this white candlewick spread by EH in 1827. The mounds were clipped to shape them more realistically. Stitches are French knots, satin, and bullion. United States; H. 103" (261.62 cm); W. 106" (269.24 cm).*

**Figure 88** *Octagonal satinwood box with elaborate sewing accessories. Cowrie shell pincushion and sewing clamp, bodkin, netting tools, needle and thimble cases, tape measure, tatting shuttle, thread, and wax holders. The heart-shaped silver tool was a knitting sheath that one pinned to one's waist to hold a knitting needle at the proper angle. The tortoise-shell case held tambour needles in assorted sizes and their holder. Author's collection.*

*here is—I can't bear to see the parlour look like a taylor's shop—beside I am going to make some important philosophical experiments . . . You must know my husband is of your wou'd be philosophers—well, I bundled up my linen as quickly as I could, and began to darn a pair of ruffles; which took up no room and could give no offence—I tho't however, I would watch my lord and master's important business."*

As it turned out, the "philosophical experiments" had a devastating effect on the parlour-turned-laboratory. The woman described the mess, and then continued archly,

*". . . tell your friend the white-wash scribbler, that this is one means by which our closets become furnished with 'halves of China bowls, cracked tumblers, broken wine glasses, tops of tea-pots and stoppers of departed decanters.' . . . I said nothing, or next to nothing; for I only observ'd very pleasantly . . . why philosophers are called literary men is because they make a great* litter. *. . .*
*I was certainly the best philosopher of the two: for my experiments succeeded [that is,* after she cleaned up after him *] and his did not. . . . My carpet, which had suffered*

FIGURE 88

*in the cause of experimental philosophy in the morning,*
*was destined to be most shamefully dishonoured in the*
*afternoon, by a deluge of nasty tobacco juice —*
*Gentlemen smoakers love segars better than carpets."*

The story (and the tirade) ended with the woman beginning her whitewashing, muttering, "The first dirty thing to be removed is one's husband." Twenty-three years before Joseph Hopkinson would pronounce women the more refined sex, this woman put it more bluntly. She called men "naturally nasty beasts; if it were not for their connection with the refined sex . . . these lords of creation would wallow in their own filth."[16]

These fighting words came from a woman who was obviously unimpressed with the Age of Enlightenment. She might have scorned the

FIGURE 89

FIGURE 90

FIGURE 91

**Figure 89** *A sewing box made in the shape of a piano. The fitted upper shelf shows its ivory and mother-of-pearl tools. The miniature piano contains a music box as well. England; 1800–25.*

**Figure 90** *Swift, or yarn winder, made of whalebone has elaborate urns and acorn finials. Made by Nathaniel Dominy V of East Hampton, Long Island; 1800–10. (Funds for purchase from the Crestlea Foundation.)*

**Figure 91** *Federal period sewing table, made in Boston, with a fitted sewing box, a heart-shaped knitting sheath, a silver chatelaine hook, scissors, and a Queen's-stitch-covered pincushion and needleholder. The silk-embroidered bag is really the lower "drawer"; 1800–10.*

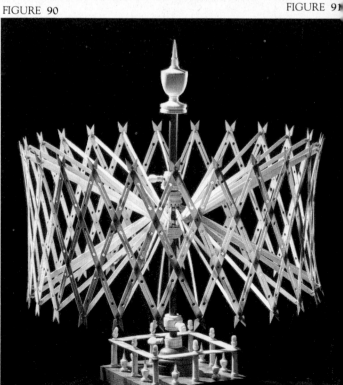

168

FIGURE 92

genteel ladies' salons as much as she did her husband's "philosophical experiments." She didn't feel demeaned as a housewife; on the contrary, she considered herself refined because she was sensible, practical, and competent. Even though denigrated by her husband, she did not question the idea of her subordination to him. She did, however, complain about it, and here she represented a dramatic break with the past. Women earlier in the century, though they shared many of her values, did not speak out as she did, at least not publicly. Here, in the spirited objections of exploited wives, were the first open skirmishes in the full-scale battle of the sexes that highlighted this period.

The climate of opinion that fostered even this modest rebellion was a result of several factors. Among the affluent especially, the rhetoric of the American and French Revolutions was absorbed into women's thinking. Orthodox religion, which previously had tended to keep women confined and submissive, lost much of its impact toward the end of the eighteenth century. Rigid religious beliefs about the inferiority of women and the depravity of children slowly softened. New liberal, humanistic influences stressed natural rights and human perfectability. These new philosophies infused the new government and its affluent constituency with unprecedented regard for women and children. Supportive men such as Benjamin Franklin and Benjamin Rush outspokenly tried to encourage women to prepare themselves to be intelligent, responsible citizens of the new republic.

The English feminist, Mary Wollstonecraft, led the struggle for women's rights. Her writings attracted a wide and distinguished readership in America, including Martha Washington. (An entry for March 31, 1794, in George Washington's account listed "*Wolstoncroft's Education* for Mrs. Washington.")[17] In particular, her 1792 book *A Vindication of the Rights of Women*, published in London, Boston, and Philadelphia, attained instant popularity and notoriety and remains today one of the most influential books ever written about women (Figure 94).

Wollstonecraft boldly asserted that men and women had equal abilities and that only society's training accounted for the disparity in their achievements. She pleaded for women to be educated in professions, rather

**Figure 92** *Trestle-base embroidery frame with adjustable side shafts for different sized needlework. Correctly stretched canvas or embroidery would have had tape sewn around all four sides and laced to the bars. New England; 1710–75.*

FIGURE 93

FIGURE 94

**Figure 93** *Empire period sewing table and an Empire sewing box resting on the writing surface. Pleated green silk taffeta lines the lid and forms the sewing bag that attaches to the underside of the table; 1810–25. Candlestick from the collection of George J. Fistrovich.*

**Figure 94** *Title page of the American edition of Mary Wollstonecraft's influential book,* A Vindication of the Rights of Woman: With Strictures on Political and Moral Subjects.

**Figure 95** *A pair of family arms, one a watercolor on paper, the other a silk embroidery on a silk satin ground, worked entirely in whipstitch. Both pieces proclaim that they represent the name of Putnam, but these arms are not recorded for Putnam or anyone else. Done by Betsy Putnam; Salem, Massachusetts; 1790–1810; H. 14 1/4" (36.20 cm); W. 10 1/8" (25.72 cm).*

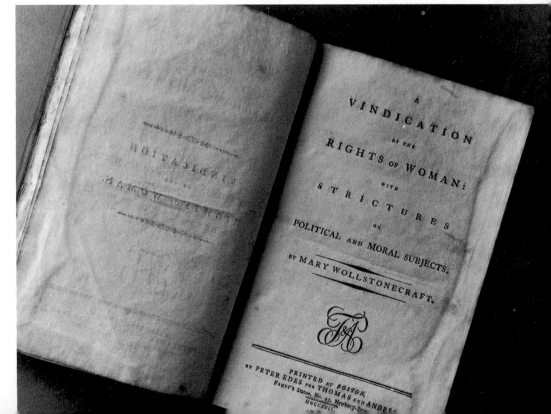

FIGURE 95

than just accomplishments, not so that they would "have power over men, but over themselves."[18] Linking the cause of women to the ideals of democracy and enlightenment, which had spurred revolutions in America and France, she observed that tyrants, whether weak fathers or kings, are always eager to crush reason. She wrote, "Do you [men] not act a similar part when you *force* all women, by denying them civil and political rights, to remain . . . groping in the dark?"[19]

She aimed directly at the ideals and rhetoric of the new American republic, rejecting a philosophy of government that proclaimed all men to be equal to each other but superior to women. "If women are to be excluded, without having a voice, from participation of the natural rights of mankind . . . [this is a] flaw in your NEW CONSTITUTION, the first constitution founded on reason," she wrote.[20]

Personal comments in letters and diaries reveal that Mary Wollstonecraft's ideas struck a nerve of truth for both men and women of the day. Elizabeth Drinker, essentially a conservative and thoughtful woman, entered in her diary of March 6, 1799, "To say the truth, I think her a prodigious fine writer—and should be charmed by some of her pieces if I had never heard her Character."[21] She agreed with many of Wollstonecraft's points but felt, "I am not for quite so much independence."[22] Unfortunately, by this time Wollstonecraft's sympathies for the French Revolution and her scandalous private life gave her the image of a dangerous radical.

A woman who called herself "A Matrimonial Republican" wrote in the July, 1792 *Ladies Magazine* that she objected to the word *obey* being part of the woman's marriage vow but not of the man's. She wrote, "Obedience between a man and wife . . . ought to be mutual." Otherwise, she concluded, the woman became a virtual slave.[23]

In August, 1792, in the same issue of the *Ladies Magazine* that favorably reviewed *A Vindication of the Rights of Women* and quoted it liberally, an article entitled "Thoughts on Women" echoed Wollstonecraft's views. The author declared, for example, "To the age of thirteen or fourteen, girls are every where superior to boys. At fourteen a boy begins to get some advantages over a girl . . . by means of education."[24]

All of these discussions and writings apparently produced at least a mild improvement in women's behavior. An unidentified "L. C." in the December, 1810 *Port Folio* noted that, "Instead of wasting precious hours of their lives in trifling amusements and petty occupations, the ladies, in a majority of instance, are now profitably employed in the cultivation of their minds. . . . The husband no longer need blush at the folly of his wife, or dread to spend the long evenings of winter in her insipid company."[25]

Real improvements for women progressed very slowly and primarily affected only women of the middling or better sort. Eager as some might have been for a new day, they had no pertinent role models to guide them. To move from a subordinate to an equal role required a great deal of change, and women had no experience in doing so. It was one thing to point out inequities but quite another to conceive of methods to change them. The typical genteel lady of the day was simply not yet ready to abandon the age-old belief, as Wollstonecraft and her followers asked her to, that nature intended men and women to have completely different roles in life. The stylish lady found the prerogatives of female privilege comforting and reassuring, and the hypothetical state of equality with men threatening and unknown. Gradually, she opted for the new exaltation men offered her—privilege, of a sort, over equality. By the 1820s, the atmosphere of unprecedented regard for women masked their new form of subservience and doomed their demands for equality. To seal the issue, men's attitudes about themselves also underwent change. The ideal of an enlightened, cultured, intellectual man gave way to the new image of man as aggressive and domineering, functioning within the competitive economic system. Men with these attitudes preferred their women exalted and obedient—above and below them, but not equal to them.

During the unprecedented period of enlightenment for women at the end of the eighteenth century and the beginning of the nineteenth century, the needlework projects of women reflected their thoughts and feelings about themselves, just as their clothing did. Other than samplers, silk needlework pictures became the most fashionable projects. To begin with, these pictures radiated elegance (Plate 39; Figure 95). Their bright, shiny silks (more readily available after the Revolution with the start of direct trade with China) complemented the new interiors, themselves more showy than before, having furniture of lighter wood, with shimmering veneered surfaces and elaborate inlays. To enhance their pictures, needleworkers added silver or gold spangles (the eighteenth-century equivalent of sequins) and metallic yarns (Figure 96). Chenille yarns contributed a plush, fuzzy texture. Glittering gold-leafed frames, often with mirrorlike black and white eglomisé mats, added the final opulent touch (Figures 97 and 98).

Though some needlework schools upheld the old standards of

FIGURE 96

FIGURE 97

**Figure 96** *Needlework picture of Maria, the heroine of Laurence Sterne's novel A Sentimental Journey. Worked with silk and a small amount of very fine wool on silk satin. Stitches are satin, whip, and chain. The chain stitch outlines the oval and holds the spaced silver spangles. Expert painting on the face and hands; the original tape that held it to the embroidery frame now laces the work to the backboard. United States; 1800–25; H. 23" (54.42 cm); W. 26 3/4" (67.95 cm).*

**Figure 97** *A flower picture finely worked in silk, using satin and whipstitches. Set with a black and gold eglomisé mat in its original frame labeled by Stillman Lothrop (an apprentice of John Doggett's; see Figures 100 and 101) of Salem, Massachusetts; H. 20 1/2" (52.07 cm); W. 16 9/16" (42.06 cm).*

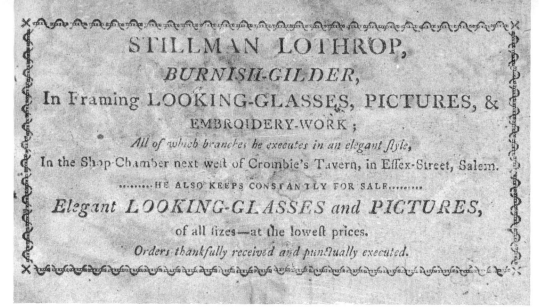

STILLMAN LOTHROP,

*BURNISH-GILDER,*

In Framing LOOKING-GLASSES, PICTURES, &

EMBROIDERY-WORK;

*All of which branches he executes in an elegant style,*

In the Shop-Chamber next west of Crombie's Tavern, in Essex-Street, Salem.

.........HE ALSO KEEPS CONSTANTLY FOR SALE.........

*Elegant LOOKING-GLASSES and PICTURES,*

of all sizes—at the lowest prices.

*Orders thankfully received and punctually executed.*

FIGURE 98

FIGURE 99

FIGURE 100

**Figure 98** *Detail of the Stillman Lothrop label. The wording on the label is evidence that many needlework pictures were framed for household decoration.*

**Figure 99** *Twelve-year-old Rachel Thaxter made this needlework picture, probably while attending the Derby Academy in Hingham, Massachusetts, in 1796. The silk background fabric was originally backed with linen fabric and the silk embroidery worked through both layers. Done in long satin, seed, and whipstitches. H. 8" (20.32 cm); W. 10 1/8" (25.73 cm)*

**Figure 100** *Picture captioned, "And the Daughter of Pharaoh came down to wash herself at the river; and when she saw the Ark among the flags she sent her maid to fetch it. Exod Ch. 2ᵈ Verse 5." On the eglomisé border in gilt letters: "Wrought by Mary S. Crafts at Mʳˢ Saunders & Miss. Beach's Academy Dorchester." The inscription on the backboard indicates that Mary was probably seventeen years old when she made this. All the solid needlework areas were done in whipstitch except the two thin trees to the left, which are satin-stitched. The faces, arms, foreground, and background were painted. 1805; H. 16 1/2" (41.91 cm); W. 12 3/4" (32.39 cm).*

179

FIGURE 101

workmanship, many needlework pictures executed around the turn of the century exhibit a gradual decline from the excellence of those from the pre-Revolutionary period (Figure 99). There are telling signs of shortcuts the needleworkers used. Especially after 1800, faces, skies, and water in many needlework pictures (and a few samplers) were painted in—an embellishment that was also a time-saver. Whereas earlier silk pictures were done in a large variety of stitches, later silk embroideries consisted primarily of rows of the quicker and easier whipstitch (Figure 100). (These pieces are often called satin-stitch pictures, but recently, during a restoration of many of them at the Henry Francis du Pont Winterthur Museum, the author discovered that what appear from the front to be satin stitches are really rows of whipstitches.)

The extravagant, often gaudy, appearance and declining workmanship of these needlework pictures show us that the lady of leisure was unwilling to do the time-consuming projects of an earlier generation. The subject matter of these pictures, however, reveals something novel. The pictures often show the new interest in classical motifs even when portraying scenes from the Bible, popular novels, or, most commonly, mourning

FIGURE 102

**Figure 101** *Account book of John Doggett for October 5, 1805, showing a bill to Mary Crafts's uncle, Eliphalet Porter, for two frames, one of $7.50 specifically for Miss Crafts's embroidery; DMMC, WM, 64x10, p. 88.*

**Figure 102** *A toy coffin of wood, complete with the glass window some people then favored for actual coffins, to be sure the body was in fact dead. This toy has a removable small carved wooden figure in it.*

scenes (Plate 36). The mourning pictures are particularly sentimental, with their long-haired maidens standing soulfully under willow trees (traditional symbols of mourning). The girls and women of this time could, and were expected to, indulge in the luxury of sentimentality. The novel, a newly accepted form of literature, depicted and accentuated these tender sentiments. The new feminine virtues included the sensitivity to be touched, even moved to tears, by tragic tales. In sharp contrast, the girls and women of the earlier era had not been encouraged to contemplate life's cruelties and display them in their crafts. Death had been dealt with directly (Figure 102). The sentimental interpretation of death or other natural occurrences was a rising new practice, spurred by the belief that the great role of art should be its impact on the imagination (Figure 77). Such sentimentality had not been previously displayed in needlework. Earlier stitched pictures had displayed bright, cheerful floral designs and scenes.

To be sure, well before needleworkers started doing mourning pictures, Americans had had elaborate mourning practices. Throughout the seventeenth and eighteenth centuries the colonists had always imbued funerals with all the pomp and ceremony they could muster. They had

FIGURE **103**

special mourning clothes and jewelry, bed hangings, window draperies, and trimmings for mirrors and portraits. There were gifts such as gold mourning rings, gloves, and handkerchiefs (Figure 103). In cities, "layers out of the dead," often women, carried a complete line of these mourning accessories. During the hard times of the Revolutionary War, there were patriotic efforts to restrict the mourning paraphernalia, in some cases to merely a black armband or ribbon for men and a black hair ribbon for women. However, after the war, the wealthy reverted to their elaborate funerals in newer, more stylish forms.

If Americans had always invested as much ceremony as possible in marking an actual death, never before had they shown such an interest in memorializing people, dead and alive. For example, in the early nineteenth century, two teachers at the Moravian School painted a large group of lively, colorful watercolors, each one featuring a different-shaped tomb, most of them topped with urns. One of these urns bears the initials of John G. Kummer, a headmaster of the school. He was still alive when it was painted, and so the dates on his urn had to be left unfinished.

It was one thing to bestow great solemnity, even ostentation, on a funeral; it was another to eulogize a person before he died. The expressions of love and esteem that in earlier, harder times had been restricted to ceremonial occasions such as funerals, now became routinely tasteful. Sentiment, and in some cases the affectation of sentiment, became stylish.

Schoolgirls were caught up in the expression of sentimentality. In 1796, Margaretta Akerly, a student at the Moravian School in Bethlehem, wrote to her sister, "It will be no trouble for me to work you a screen [probably a fire screen covering]. I shall do it with the utmost pleasure; I think it will look best on white sattin . . . But I wish you to chuse a Motto to go in the Urn. If you wish a name let me know and I will do it."[26] Obviously the Akerly mourning piece owed its inspiration strictly to fashion rather than to any personal reason for mourning. Similarly, when Eliza Southgate's sister Octavia wrote from Mrs. Rowson's school at Medford, Massachusetts, asking her sister to help select her next needlework project, Eliza replied "About your work . . . a *mourning piece* with a figure in it, and two other pictures, *mates*—figures of females I think

*Figure 103  A group of mourning pins and rings, for the fashionable display of grief. The coffin-shaped spoon handle became popular during the long period of public mourning observed for George Washington, 1800–10. The Irish-stitched Bible in the background was worked in shades of red, blue, purple, and gold and once belonged to the Philadelphia cabinetmaker John Gillingham. It was probably stitched by his wife, Ann, or daughter Elizabeth. (Three of the mourning rings were the gift of Mrs. George Batchelder. The Washington hair pin was the gift of Mrs. Paul Hammond.)*

handsomer than Landscapes."[27]

George Washington's death, in 1799, provoked a wave of mourning that took many forms. American needleworkers and other craftsmen produced a flood of mourning pictures in honor of Washington, and the President who when he lived had taken pains not to be treated as a king became instead somewhat sanctified when he died. Few homes in America were without a print, needlework picture, or some other representation of Washington's death. Mourning had become patriotic as well as stylishly sensitive (Figures 104 and 105).

Perhaps Mark Twain best summarized this style of sentimentality in *Huckleberry Finn*. By the time Twain was writing, in the last third of the nineteenth century, mourning pictures had gone out of style, but apparently they had made a lasting impression. In one scene Huck confronted a room full of mourning pictures, one of which memorialized even the demise of a bird. Taken aback, Huck reasoned that the person responsible for decorating the room had gloried in her "tributes" to the dead, but he confessed that they only gave him "the fantods."[28]

Paradoxically, these silk mourning pictures embraced classical symbolism while they indulged in romantic sentimentality. Compositions featuring mourners at a graveside harken back to antiquity (Virgil had presented a mourning theme in "Tomb of Arcadia" in the Fifth Eclogue). A few mourning themes with a tomb, weeping willows, and classically clad figures were used in needlework, memorial jewelry, and prints in America in the 1790s, prior to Washington's death.[29] However, the great emphasis on creating mourning objects occurred between 1800 and 1830. Fashionable women adopted the classical custom of memorializing the dead with tombs and urns, transforming these receptacles of honor into monuments to sentimentality.

The position of women changed during these years, with the exuberant optimism of the revolutionary age receding while a more restrictive, sentimental outlook on life set in. Perhaps the popularity of needlework mourning pictures conveys some awareness on the part of this class of women of their altered status. Put another way, women buried the idea of their enlightenment in its own symbols.

**Plate 37** *Sarah Wentworth Apthrop Morton (1759–1846) of Boston, in her early forties, painted by Gilbert Stuart. She was a member of Boston's elite society, both by birth and her marriage to Perez Morton. She took full advantage of the few years of women's enlightenment to publish her poetry, articles, and books.*

FIGURE 104

FIGURE 105

**Figure 104** *The centered tomb design of this mourning picture was traced exactly from Figure 105. The skillful silk embroiderer used whip, satin, French knots, and seed stitches. The faces, arms, and sky were rather poorly painted on the silk. Washington's picture was painted on paper and appliquéd to the tomb. A linen strip, with eyelet holes, that was used to lace the embroidery in a sewing frame is still attached. United States; 1800–10; H. 15 1/4″ (38.74 cm); W. 16 3/4″ (42.55 cm).*

**Figure 105** *Etching titled "Pater Patriae" by Enoch G. Gridley, based on a painting by John Coles, Jr. The portrait medallion of George Washington was copied from the one painted by Edward Savage. 1800; H. 13 1/2″ (34.29 cm); W. 9 1/2″ (24.13 cm).*

**Figure 106** *Picture of the Franklin Marble Mantel Manufactory in Philadelphia, located on Race Street between Sixth and Seventh Streets, about 1830. From Thomas Porter's* Picture of Philadelphia *from 1811 to 1831, published in Philadelphia by Robert Desilver in 1831. DMMC, WM, F158.44P54me, v 2.*

FIGURE 106

PLATE 38

PLATE 39

**Plate 38** *A mahogany paint box and a page from an album owned by Eleutheria du Pont Smith. Young girls often displayed their painting accomplishment by doing watercolor pictures accompanied by original verses in their friends' scrapbooks. The poem preceding this picture is signed by Clemintina B. Smith, August 28, 1829. The Marquis de Lafayette wrote in the front of this book when he visited Wilmington on July 25, 1825. DMMC, WM, 65x623.1.*

**Plate 39** *A bunch of flowers realistically portrayed in a meticulously worked silk embroidery on white satin. It is still in its original frame labeled by Stillman Lothrop of Salem, Massachusetts, with a black and gold, eglomisé border. Boston–Salem; 1790–1820; H. 19" (48.26 cm); W. 16 3/16" (41.12 cm).*

189

# 5 To Make a House a Home
## *The Age of Domesticity*

FIGURE 107

Sentimental, genteel, and too unsure of themselves to press their earlier claims of equality with men, American women wound up on a less-than-honorable pedestal, glorified for their refinement but firmly limited to a life of domesticity, self-sacrifice, and submission. Instead of gaining power "over themselves," as Wollstonecraft had urged, women assumed the position of moral guardian of the family and allowed this elevated status to mask their continued inferior position. Society righteously insisted that the natures of men and women differed widely and that therefore their roles should be separate and distinct. Women accepted this view. They sought and received praise for their supposedly unique virtues of passivity, delicacy, obedience, patience, and moral purity, whereas men were lauded for their strength, aggression, and sense of adventure. An unpublished diary of a young Boston woman in 1827 professed that "the sphere of a woman's usefulness ought to be chiefly confined to her family and friends." [1] While the typical husband was active, participating in the outside world, his wife operated in a passive sphere of domesticity.

This role for women was rooted in the social and economic practices of the dawning industrial age. Even before the start of the nineteenth century, the urban husband's place of employment began to move outside the home. When it did, the woman of the house could no longer function as her husband's partner in the closely linked home and business affairs of the family, and thereby gain a limited parity with him. The new economic system separated the home from the business and the husband from his wife. The man became the provider, the woman the homemaker, almost literally.

The post-colonial period of enlightenment had softened these new restrictions by permitting women to loosen their ties to the home without breaking them. However, as the commercial ferment of industrial development overwhelmed the cultural sensibilities of the Age of Enlightenment, women were thrust back into the home again. Man assumed the role of a warrior in the working world who depended on his wife to prepare a sanctuary for him. Woman, with her refinement and sensitivity, was deemed not only well-suited for the task of haven-making but ennobled by it. In her home she reigned over children, virtue, faith, taste—all things

**Figure 107** *Purse and eyeglass case using merino yarns in the Irish stitch. Purse: United States; 1830–70; H. 6 1/8" (15.57 cm); W. 6 1/2" (16.51 cm). Eyeglass case; H. 6 1/8" (15.57 cm); W. 2" (5.08 cm).*

192

that, like herself, had little or no place in a man's world of business.

The Second Great Awakening, an evangelical religious movement that swept the United States early in the nineteenth century, helped create this new role for women. The clergy so assiduously cultivated women with praise for their moral virtues that Mrs. Frances Trollope, the caustic English travel writer, observed, ". . . it is from the clergy only that women of America receive the sort of attention which is so dearly valued by every young female heart throughout the world." [2]

Meanwhile, the clergy rarely reached men, who considered themselves too busy earning a living to be vitally concerned with moral preachments. Mrs. Trollope observed, "I never saw, or read, of any country where religion had so strong a hold upon the women, or a slighter hold upon the men." [3]

The press joined the pulpit in its crusade to appoint women society's moral guardians. Women in America had never lacked instruction from printed materials on how to behave, but after 1830, this material greatly increased, spurred by the growing literacy rate among women, an increase in their leisure time, and the invention of lower-cost printing machinery. Spiritual sustenance became available to women of all economic levels via newspapers, manner books, and magazines. The pioneer magazine in ladies' how-to literature, *The Lady's Book*, started in 1830 by Louis A. Godey and soon known as *Godey's Lady's Book*, offered among other items short moralistic stories and the editorial exhortations of its editor, Sarah Josepha Hale. Other such magazines as *Miss Leslie's Magazine* and *Miss Peterson's National Magazine* soon chimed in.

Even daily newspapers served as advisers to women. On November 28, 1827, a "Code of Instructions for Ladies" in the *Baltimore American and Commercial Daily Advertiser* summarized society's expectations of its women:

> 1. *Let every wife be persuaded that there are two ways of governing a family; the first is by the expression of that will which belongs to force; the second by the power of mildness. One is the power of the husband; the wife should never employ any other arms than gentleness.*

FIGURE 108

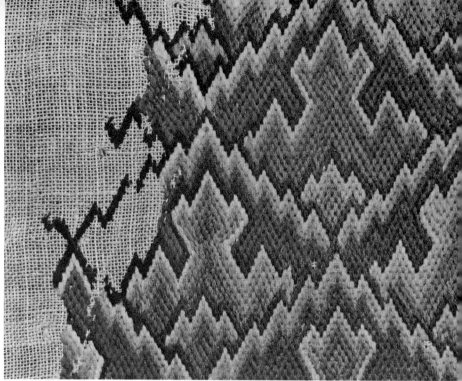

FIGURE 109

2. *Avoid contradicting your husband.* . . .

3. *Occupy yourself only with your household affairs.* . . .

4. *Never take upon yourself to be a censor of your husband's morals.* . . .

5. *Command his attention by being always attentive to him.*

6. *All men are vain, never wound this vanity.* . . . *A wife may have more sense than her husband, but she should never seem to know it.*

7. *When a man gives wrong counsel, never make him feel that he has done so.* . . .

8. *When a husband is out of temper, behave obligingly to him.* . . .

9. *Choose well your female friends; have but few.* . . .

10. *Cherish neatness without luxury, and pleasure without excess; dress with taste, and particularly with modesty.* . . .

11. *Never be curious to pry into your husband's concerns.* . . .

FIGURE 110

12.  *Seem always to obtain information from him, especially before company, though you may pass yourself for a simpleton. Never forget that a wife owes all her importance to that of her husband. —Leave him entirely master of his actions, to go and come whenever he thinks fit.*

A woman had always been considered a jewel in her husband's crown. Now she found herself expected to be his benefactress as well, restraining herself and even practicing deceit to cater to his sense of superiority. She had little other choice, for she depended on her husband more than ever. She was his to honor or exploit. In the editorial "Advice to a Bride" in *The Lady's Book* for May, 1832, Sarah Hale warned, "Your duty is submission. . . . Your husband is, by the laws of God and of man, your superior; do not ever give him a cause to remind you of it."[4]

Sometimes a woman attempted to make an asset of her dependence, flattering her husband with her vulnerability, but this was a dangerous ploy. Frances Wright, a perceptive Englishwoman who visited America, found that men thought it pleasing to have as "their companion a fragile vine,

PLATE 40

**Plate 40**  *The giving of a quilting party, especially in rural areas, was similar in purpose to an engagement announcement today. This unsigned painting, by J. [John] L. [Lewis] KRIMMEL PINX/PHIL*[A]. *1813 illustrates that after the quilt had been finished the invited guests and future bridegroom arrived to enjoy a dinner and perhaps dancing.*

**Plate 41**  *A large appliquéd quilt using English roller-printed chintzes of the 1830s. The quilting itself, done in a very fine running stitch, creates a texture. United States; 1835–45; H. 123″ (312.42 cm); W. 118 3/4″ (299.72 cm).*

PLATE **41**

clinging to their firm trunk for support." Yet these same vines, she realized, often "weighed the oak to the ground."[5] Women had to be submissive without being burdensome, a delicate balance to maintain.

Girls who had grown up with the romantic expectation that in marriage they would be completely cared for by men had to learn how to cultivate this privileged state. The life of a woman developed into an unending mission to endear herself to her husband, to "preserve a perpetual charm," as Mrs. Hale put it, for "the nature of man is such, that where there is no excitement, there he is faithless. . . . The ardour of man's dispositions leads him to very romantic professions . . . without doubt sincerely intended—but he professes more than humanity can accomplish."[6]

To allow her husband to feel free and yet to keep him coming back to her, a wife strived to give him what he wanted and to make as few demands on him as possible. She was admonished not to meddle in his affairs —not to burden him in any way because he already carried the burdens of

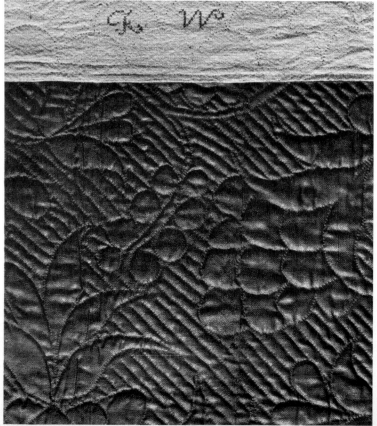

FIGURE 111

**Figure 111** *A one-piece quilt with indigo glazed wool in a twill weave with a gold plain-woven wool lining. Fine running stitches created the flowers and grapes rambling over the surface. Initialed R W in cross-stitch. America; 1780–1800; H. 97" (246.38 cm); W. 81" (205.74 cm).*

**Figure 112** *One-piece quilted petticoat, made of pink silk satin has exotic flowers stitched in very fine running stitches. Originally owned by a member of the Barker family of Scituate, Massachusetts. H. 36 3/4" (93.35 cm); W. around hem 110 1/2" (280.67 cm).*

FIGURE 112

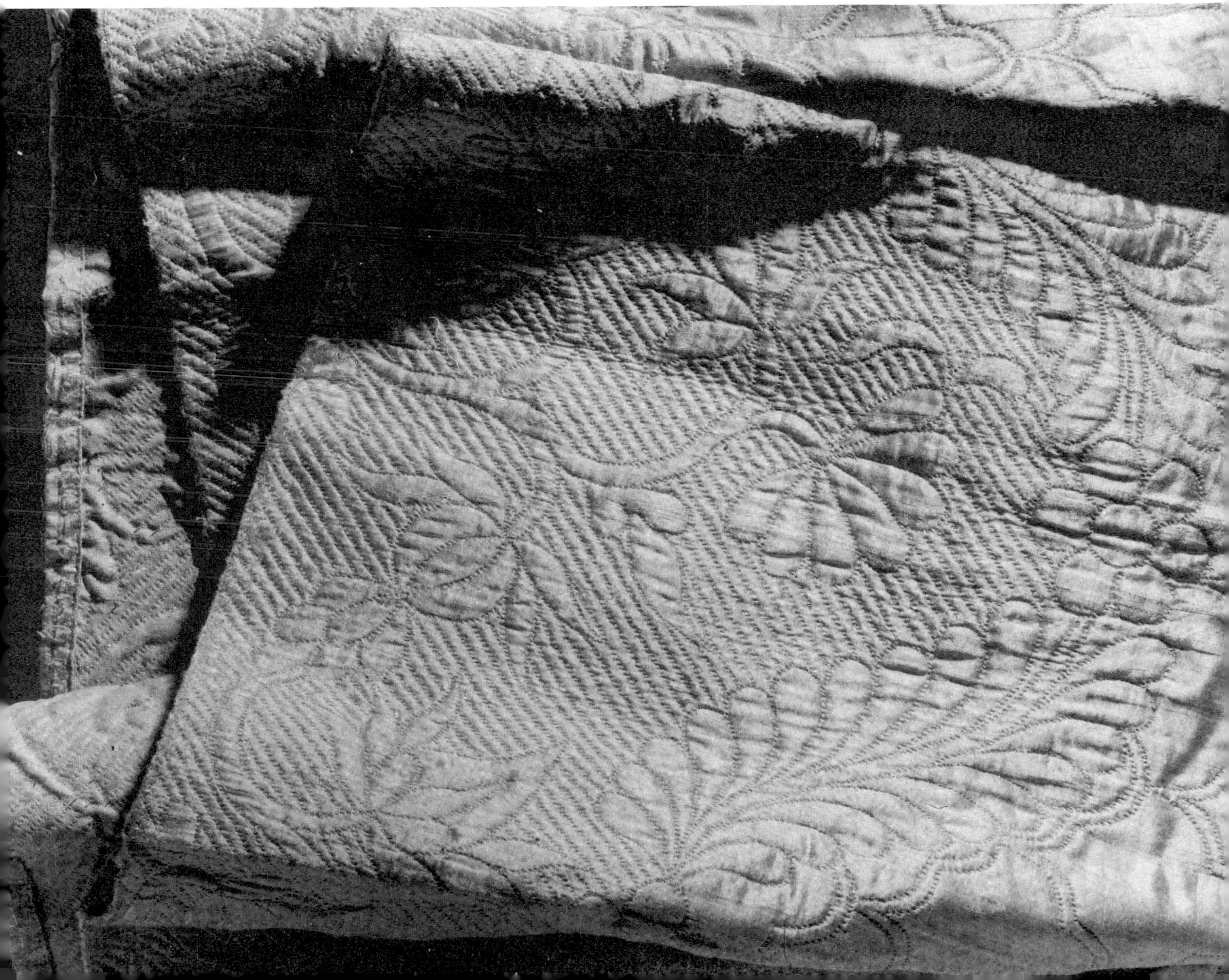

PLATE 42

**Plate 42** A quilt that displays a combination of techniques: the diamonds are pieced; the pots of flowers are appliquéd, and there are many embroidered accents in crewel yarns. United States; 1810–40; H. 74" (197.95 cm); W. 61" (154.94 cm).

business. He wanted a tranquil refuge from the worries of the working world, and she was to devote herself to creating it. Mrs. Hale counseled, "Let all your enjoyment centre in your home. Let your home occupy the first place in your thoughts; for that is the only source of happiness."[7]

To be sure, a few women, especially those who had received good educations, did choose the alternative to the life of a housewife. Against great odds and adversity, they pursued careers, usually at the cost of being all but ostracized by society. There was often no middle ground of having both a family and a profession. Victorian society considered homemaking a woman's highest calling, and for the society to have permitted women both marriage and a career would have implied that homemaking was less than totally fulfilling. If she chose a career, a woman had to be prepared to sacrifice marriage and a family, and, like spinsters all through the years, endure ridicule.

In professional life, the few exceptions needed skill, endurance, courage, and luck to succeed. Elizabeth Blackwell, the first female medical student in the country, managed to gain admittance to Geneva College in New York, when the administrators, taken aback by an application from a female, decided to poll the student body to determine whether a woman should be accepted. The students refused to believe that a woman was really applying and, thinking it all a joke, voted to admit her.

Of the overwhelming majority of women who remained in the home, some aspired to a semiprofessional level of competence in their homemaking, stimulated by the teachings of such leading educators as Catherine Beecher. She stressed the importance of the family as the foundation of the social order. Women, by promoting the happiness and well-being of the family, helped shape a virtuous society.[8] Her 1841 *Treatise on Domestic Economy* gave clear, sensible advice on all facets of homemaking, including even the architectural design of the house. Her practical approach did more to elevate the status of the housewife than all the flowery rhetoric about women's virtues. However, on the whole, sentimentality and a new womanly virtue—propriety—overwhelmed practicality and competence as ideals for women.

The Victorian lady's activities outside the home centered on church

FIGURE 113

activities, visiting, and shopping. The wife continued and in many cases expanded her rounds of visiting. Calling was no longer always done for the gaiety of it—it had become almost a chore—but to uphold her social position and, by inevitable extension, that of her husband. The calling cards she left behind served, according to *The Young Lady's Friend* (1837), "to keep up a ceremonious acquaintance with a circle too large for friendly visiting, as that consumes far more time than could be given to the number of persons you must be acquainted with."⁹

The busy husband turned over much of the household purchasing to his wife. Diaries and contemporary remarks show that shopping (not necessarily purchasing) became a pastime for many of these idle women. Servants became essential to supply the leisure time for shopping and visiting. Husbands, even if they could barely afford it, often felt obliged by their social position to hire at least a cook and maid for the household.

**Figure 113** *A one-piece quilt created from a once brilliantly colored, Indian hand-painted and resist-dyed printed fabric. In one corner is the original stamp of the English East India Company on the fabric. The quilt was owned by the Augustine Boyer family of Kent County, Maryland. 1700–60; H. 111 1/4″ (282.57 cm); W. 87 1/2″ (222.25 cm). (Gift of Miss Gertrude Brinkle.)*

**Figure 114** *Pieced silk quilt made of wide vertical bands of fabric in a pleasing variety of grays, gray green, and gold. Quilting is finely done in the running stitch. Lining of brown cotton. Belonged to a Quaker family in Chester County, Pennsylvania. 1750–1820; H. 102″ (259.08 cm); W. 105 1/4″ (267.33 cm).*

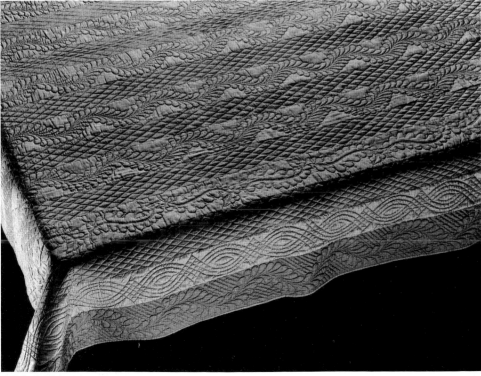

FIGURE 114

FIGURE 115

Management of this help added another necessary skill to the new domesticity.

Victorian housewives with time to fill, hands to keep busy, and homes to prettify became zealous needleworkers. They made innumerable household accessories, covering anything that didn't move, and a few things that did—slippers, wastebaskets, ottomans, picture frames, cigar cases, pillows, tables, bellpulls, needle cases, and antimacassars. And now —again thanks to the less-expensive printing machinery—almost every woman could learn to do fancy needlework. No longer did women need special tutoring from needlework teachers. The same magazines that a woman relied on for guidance about fitting behavior plied her with needlework patterns and instructions for projects that were all well within the capabilities of the average housewife.

Starting in the 1840s, needlework books also began to appear en masse, further popularizing fancy needlework. From posterity's standpoint, these books made their greatest contribution in further obfuscating needlework terminology, as if it were not already confusing enough. Probably in an effort to distinguish their books from those of the competition, the authors took to making tiny variations on well-known stitches and then renaming the stitches, often with elegant-sounding foreign names. Sometimes they simply changed the name of a stitch without bothering to change the stitch itself.

The great vogue in needlework during the Victorian period was Berlin work, a form that took its name from the fact that, about 1804, a printseller in Berlin, A. Philipson, originated it. Philipson had the idea of making paper with many intersecting lines (similar to graph paper) to correspond to a canvas background. He then had the designs hand painted on this paper for the needleworker to copy onto her canvas. She could transfer the design, square for square, in whatever stitch she chose—usually cross or tent but occasionally Irish. She didn't even have to bother with color selection, or "shading," as needlework instructors had called it, because the paper pattern came already colored (Figure 108). (A similar form, intended primarily for knitting, with printed symbols for the different colors, appeared late in the eighteenth century. However, these books carried instructions only in German and were uncommon, if they were available at all, in America.)

Berlin work became so popular that the manufacturers of canvases adapted their products to it, using a white, yellow, or blue thread every tenth space on the canvas to enable the needlewoman to count squares more easily and thus transfer the design from the pattern more quickly (Figure 109). Another innovation in canvas, developed in the mid-nineteenth century and still popular today, is Penelope, or Berlin. It consists of doubled warp and weft threads, which allow the needleworker to separate the paired threads and thereby fashion a double fine mesh. However, in general, background canvases became coarser than they had been in the eighteenth century. One rarely finds Victorian canvas work finer than twenty-four holes to the inch. It was, after all, not by demanding fine

**Figure 115** *Mary Ann Hoyt of Reading, Pennsylvania, dated this simple pieced quilt May 15, 1834. Allover stenciled coverlets are not rare, but it is uncommon to find a quilt such as this one, in which hand-stenciled squares are included among the printed textiles. The plain diagonal quilting lines were done in the running stitches. H. 86 1/2" (219.71 cm); W. 73" (185.42 cm).*

FIGURE 116

**Figure 116** *A simple repeating design and dramatically vivid color combination created a bold quilt. Cotton and wool fabrics were mixed to make the orange red border, surrounded by green diamonds with two shades of blue and red. Lined in mustard-colored cotton. Cross-stitched script markings on one edge of the border are C M A and 1834. United States; H. 173 1/4" (442.60 cm); W. 174 1/2" (443.23 cm).*

**Figure 117** *Meticulously pieced quilt formed from a series of ellipses joined in a circular design. A tricky technique worked by Fanny Johnson of Frederick, Maryland, from six different glazed, English, roller-printed chintzes of the 1830s. The lining is of plain white cotton and has two stenciled seals of the BOOTT MILLS/LOWELL factory in Massachusetts. 1830–50; H. 121 7/8" (309.50 cm); W. 116 1/4" (295.00 cm). (Gift of Mrs. John W. Avirett.)*

workmanship that Berlin work established its popularity. Its appeal lay rather in its convenience, like other products of the Industrial Revolution. It did require patience but very little skill and no creativity. Victorian women distinguished themselves by the quantity rather than the quality of their needlework. In 1840, in her book *The Art of Needle-Work from Earliest Times,* the Countess of Wilton wrote, "Of the fourteen thousand Berlin patterns which have been published, [in the ten years since 1830] scarcely one-half are moderately good."[10]

Before 1830, most American needlewomen used regular crewel or silk yarns, sometimes combined with beads, to work the printed Berlin patterns. After 1830, softer, angoralike merino yarns, gradually found their way into Berlin work and samplers. Between 1800 and 1810, the United States witnessed a fad for merino sheep, and the price of purebred sheep rose sharply. Domestic yarns became available soon afterward, but for quite some time they did not gain a competitive advantage over imported yarns (Figure 107).

In dyeing merino yarns, the Germans at first outshone the British, who previously had always been the wool specialists. Thus the yarns came to be called "Berlin," "German," or "zephyr" wools. An entry from the Moravian School in Bethlehem, Pennsylvania, discloses that even this school, famous for its fine fancy needlework, succumbed to Berlin work's overwhelming popularity. In 1839, John G. Kummer purchased for the school "Zephyr" yarn, canvas, and patterns by number from the New York City firm A. S. Schrader.[11]

The most popular yarns were of vivid colors, made even more intense after the invention of the synthetic dye aniline in 1858. Many of these new dyes proved very fugitive, and as a result many pieces of Berlin

FIGURE 117

work that survive today have changed color and faded badly, leaving us only pale renditions of the strident color schemes that were considered fashionable during the mid-nineteenth century. Strong maroons, purples, pinks, and oranges clashed with equally strong greens and blues. The Countess of Wilton wrote that Berlin work "seems to have been [meant] to produce a glare of colour rather than the subdued but beautiful effect" of the Gobelin tapestries that this work was meant to imitate.[12]

Later in the nineteenth century, Mark Twain wrote about Berlin work with some irreverence. In *Life on the Mississippi,* he described a needlework picture of " 'Washington Crossing the Delaware' . . . done in thunder-and-lightning crewels by one of the young ladies—work of art which would have made Washington hesitate about crossing, if he could have foreseen what advantage was going to be taken of it."[13]

In addition to depictions of historical events, Berlin-work designs of scenes from the Bible and Shakespeare—all calling for similarly gaudy color schemes—also sold well. The Victorian woman had a taste for sentimentality that was more pronounced than that of her predecessors. Doing needlework to enhance a serene little nest for herself and her family, she naturally favored designs that promoted this rose-colored view of the world. Mottos such as "God bless this home" often added the final, precious touch to her needlework.

In time, this needlework, like the life it epitomized, often became more stultifying than rewarding. Not even the continued urgings of the magazines, hinting that yet another trifle would further sanctify her place in the home, could keep the housewife producing Berlin work indefinitely. By 1860 or 1870, the great quantity and low quality of such work in most homes became the subject of derisive magazine articles, and women tried to find new ways to demonstrate their devotion to their homes.

At least one escape could provide a reliable respite from the tedium of domesticity—the company of other women. Many women drawn to the religious reawakening and pietistic movements for solace, inspiration, and support also found satisfaction in the ensuing companionship and interaction with other women. This sort of socializing ought not to be confused with the perfunctory social calls of the time, in which women used each other to keep up appearances. Here women had the chance to form meaningful friendships in an atmosphere of Christian kindliness and charity. Around the start of the nineteenth century, men's and women's interests had converged, allowing women a tentative foothold in the male social world. Now thoroughly excluded from the male world, women opted for the company of other women as a relief from the burdens of marriage and motherhood. Women had always sought each other out, but now they had a greater need for their companionship than ever before.

A different but equally satisfying reason to congregate came on the occasions when a woman was ready to finish a quilt. Quilting, one of the more creative forms of early American needlework, was a form that readily lent itself to numerous hands and festive affairs (Plate 40). An invitation to a quilting party often signified the engagement of the hostess. The bride-to-be would invite her female friends to help her put the finishing touches on quilt tops that she had been preparing for her future home. At the end of the day or days of quilting, the local young men arrived for a meal and perhaps dancing. Then they escorted the young women home. Women would bring small pieces of their quilt tops with them to work on while visiting. The many hours required to stitch the top to its interlining and backing allowed women lengthy, unhurried times together, during which they could share their feelings and strengthen their friendships. Quilt making did not begin in the Victorian era any more than the socializing it encouraged among women. But like the socializing, quilting attained its greatest importance during this period.

The first settlers brought quilted petticoats to the colonies from England, and the women who first sewed quilts here made adaptations of those from their homeland. During the eighteenth century, quilt making flourished along with all the other forms of needlework. During the nineteenth century, home quilt making increased among women of all social levels, except among well-to-do women, who could afford to buy ready-made quilts. The women of the middling sort produced most of our surviving quilts, "show" quilts, which have lasted because they were saved for company, whereas the more common utility quilts that people would regularly use for warmth eventually wore out. The appliquéd "friendship

FIGURE **118**

quilts," which come from this era, are some of the most interesting quilts
to be found today.

Quilting is the process of sewing together three separate layers of
fabric—the top, the filling, and the lining (Figure 110). The filling is usually
cotton batting, called "cotton-wool," or occasionally, it is simply a worn
blanket. The nature of the top layer determines the type of quilt—one-
piece, pieced, or appliquéd.

Quilts with one-piece tops were the earliest made in America.
Usually their ornamentation derived not so much from the fabric as from
the design and the fineness of the stitches fastening the three layers together
(Figure 111). During the eighteenth century, women quilted petticoats in
this style, the finest ones being made of silk (Figure 112). Elizabeth Drinker,
for example, recorded on August 26, 1763, that she had "put a Gown skirt
in ye Frame, to Quilt this Afternoon." Four days later she added, "Sister
and self finish'd my Quilt this afternoon."[14] (Quilting frames were relatively
inexpensive. Because they occupied much space, they were usually left up

only when in use.) Bodices, jackets, and coats (for both men and women) are other examples of items made using one-piece quilting. Once in a while, the one-piece top consisted of a fabric with a printed pattern, such as an Indian tree of life, instead of a plain-colored fabric. In these cases the seamstress usually decided not to compete with the dominant design and joined the layers together in a simple diamond or a chevron pattern (Figure 113), instead of the customary elaborate stitching.

The second type of quilt, often a utility quilt, is the pieced quilt. The seamstress aligned the edge of adjacent shapes cut from fabric, stitched them with a running stitch near the edges, and then pressed the raw edges toward the filling layer. Pieced quilting was not a difficult process if the edges of the pieces were straight (Figures 114, 115 and 116); curved pieces

FIGURE 119

**Figure 118** *A trundle bed with a silk pieced quilt. This quilt contains a variety of woven, embroidered, yarn-dyed, and hand-painted fabrics. Each piece was first backed with a piece of newspaper. Some show dates of 1788, 1789, and 1790. The paper stiffener made it easier to work with small pieces of silk. Attributed to Martha Agry Vaughn of Hallowell, Maine; 1800–20; II. 100" (254.00 cm); W. 104" (264.16 cm).*

**Figure 119** *Margaret Nichols is said to have made this quilt as a wedding present for her sister, Hannah. The quilt is signed H N, 1813. The diamond and triangular shapes were pieced, whereas the birds, foliage, and swags were appliquéd. The working of the vines and grapes in one border resembles the technique used for a one-piece quilt. Probably Delaware; H. 101" (256.54 cm); W. 91" (231.14 cm). (Gift of Mr. and Mrs. William Elkington.)*

211

were apt to stretch out of shape when sewn, making the task more vexing (Figure 117).

Naturally enough, the best clues to the date and origin of a pieced quilt come from the fabrics used. The early pieced quilt in Figure 118 is a virtual textile sample book for the period from 1780 to 1800.

On an appliquéd quilt the top layer of the quilt is embellished by either applying material to it or, in the most exacting quilting technique, called inlaid work, cutting away parts of the top layer and stitching contrasting-color pieces underneath in their places. In the earliest form of appliqué work, the needlewoman cut out designs from a printed fabric— a bird, for example—leaving one-quarter- to one-eighth-inch margins around the figure. She then turned under the margins of the cutout pieces to prevent raveling and arranged the pieces on a large background fabric, which would become the top layer of the quilt. Finally, she affixed the pieces to the background fabric with a blind whipstitch (Figure 119), or a decorative stitch such as the chain or buttonhole stitch (Figure 120). In the late nineteenth century this technique acquired the name broderie perse.

Some of the especially adept early quilters created an interesting texture by embroidering the background areas between the appliquéd pieces so finely and tautly that these sections appear delicately puckered (Plate 41).

In a similar, though later, nineteenth-century form of appliqué quilting, the needleworker determined the shape of the cutout herself, rather than adopting a design from a fabric. She used a paper or tin pattern, in the shape of a star, for example, usually favoring plain-colored fabrics or very even, tiny prints. Again she left margins around the cutout pieces, folded the edges underneath to prevent raveling, and stitched the pieces to a background fabric, usually with a blind whipstitch, thus completing the top layer of her quilt. Friendship quilts, usually made from appliqué work of this type, combined the squares of cutout material from many different seamstresses, each of whom inked or stitched her name into the part she contributed (Figure 121).

Often a quilt that appears to have been made from just one

*Figure 120 A quilt displaying a variety of techniques: embroidered accents, pieced triangles and bands, appliquéd flowers and figures, and stuffed and corded foliage and flowers. In the center scene, blue silk and beige linen threads have been used to appliqué the figures and tree in several variations of the buttonhole stitch. United States; 1820–34; H. 82 3/4" (210.19 cm); W. 96" (243.84 cm).*

212

FIGURE 120

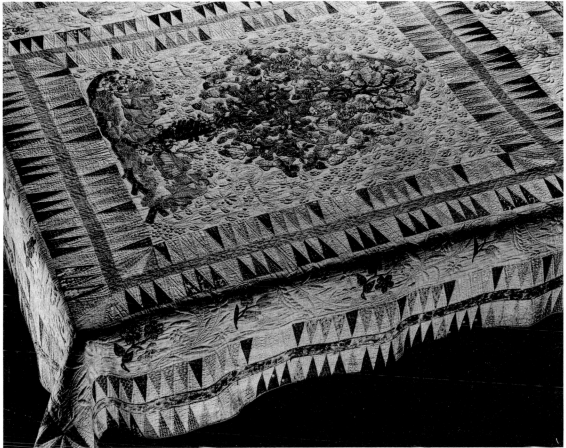

technique reveals several others on closer inspection (Plate 42). Most of these techniques were so common to our forebearers that if a woman mentioned them at all she did not distinguish between them, for example between pieced and appliqué work. However, inlaid work, because it was so intricate, did merit special mention by name, as when William Obryen in the *Georgia Gazette* for November 2, 1774, offered "FORTY SHILLINGS REWARD—Stolen . . . A BED QUILT . . . the middle a large tree (inlaid work) with a peacock at the root." In the nineteenth and twentieth centuries women gave names to different designs, but unfortunately, these names often varied from region to region, which resulted in a confusing nomenclature.

Sometimes women used the pieced or appliqué technique for small projects such as pockets or pictures, never intending to quilt them (Figure

*213*

123). For instance, the dresses in the mourning picture in Figure 77 are black appliquéd silk. The picture in Figure 122 may have been worked purely for decoration, or perhaps it was originally intended for a quilt center.

With a few exceptions, such as inlaid work, quilting, like Berlin work, was simple even though time-consuming. Most quilts were done with just the basic running stitch; very few included many of the fancywork embroidery stitches. But unlike the strictly decorative Berlin work, quilts served practical functions. Old ones were sometimes hung in doorways and windows to cut down on drafts, or suspended from attic or lean-to beams

FIGURE 121

**Figure 121** *Appliquéd "autograph" quilt from Harrison, New York, dated 1857. One girl added padding under the apple and cherry sprigs (next to the pineapple square) to puff them up. Some names are stitched in the cross- and backstitch; others are written in ink. H. 68" (172.72 cm); W. 78" (198.12 cm).*

**Figure 122** *Appliquéd scene thought to be a rendering of the flight into Egypt by the Holy Family as depicted by an early nineteenth-century woman. Perhaps intended to be the center of a quilt, but never finished. Owned by the Warner family of New York and Connecticut; 1810–30; H. 40 5/8" (103.20 cm); W. 40 3/4" (103.50 cm).*

FIGURE **122**

FIGURE 123

as room dividers. In 1835, the inventory of Susan Ward showed that she owned "1 [pair of] dimity quilt curtains."[15] According to John Fanning Watson, quilts served to delineate market stalls on fair days in Philadelphia.

Also unlike Berlin work, which was basically copy stitching, quilts allowed the needleworker to be creative, almost a forgotten word among women in the Victorian era. Some quilts display delicate and refined taste in their subtle blending of colors and prints; others are vigorous and bold, with large pieces and almost clashing color schemes. All captured something of the individual personality of the maker. The considerable amount of time it took to make a quilt gave a woman reason to associate some very personal feelings with it. She might have done one part of it while awaiting the birth of a baby, another while a son was off to war, and these personal experiences could return to her as she looked at the finished product. Quilts were no paeans to sentimentality; they were chronicles of real life.

It is ironic that quilts represent an era in the history of American women that was on the whole as repressive as the quilts themselves were creative. The progress of women in America has not been continuous or without setbacks, and the Victorian age produced at least as many setbacks as advances.

Victorian propriety made it less likely that a woman would consume herself in continual child bearing, but Victorian industrial "progress" forced many poorer women into factories where gruesome working conditions consumed them almost as brutally. Among those women whose husbands' wealth allowed them to stay in the home, the Beechers, the Susan B. Anthonys, and their followers were the rare, able exceptions. The strictures of Victorian society encapsulated women's abilities, which the previous age had just begun to recognize. Painstakingly, women would rediscover and expand their vision of what they could do and would be. In the process, however, most fancy needlework lost its preeminent place as women's most creative mode of expression. The product of a simpler, pre-industrial age, fancy needlework was practically smothered in the Victorian years of domesticity. Later generations of women, perhaps in admiration of what their colonial forebears had wrought, revived the skills, creatively adapting stitches and designs to contemporary purposes.

**Figure 123**  *A pair of pockets pieced together, probably from leftover scraps. Lined in linen and initialed in fine cross-stitches, as good household linen was supposed to be. America; 1780–1810; 15 7/8 (40.34 cm); 12 1/4" (31.12 cm).*

# Notes

## Introduction

1. Benjamin Rush, "Thoughts upon Female Education . . . ," *The Universal Asylum and Columbian Magazine* (May, 1790), p. 292.

2. Diary of Mehetable May Dawes, June 21, 1815, Schlesinger Library, Radcliffe College, Cambridge, Mass.

## Chapter 1

1. Eliza Southgate Bowne, *A Girl's Life Eighty Years Ago* (New York: Charles Scribner's Sons, 1887), p. 10.

2. Rebecca Franks to her sister Abigail, August 10, 1781, "Letter of Miss Rebecca Franks," *The Pennsylvania Magazine of History and Biography*, 23, no. 3 (1899), p. 307.

3. Diary of Elizabeth Drinker, June 20, 1795, Historical Society of Pennsylvania, Philadelphia.

4. Sarah Anna Emery, *Reminiscences of a Nonagenarian* (Newburyport, Mass.: William H. Huse & Co., 1879), p. 8.

5. *Observations sur les Moeurs &c. des Habitans de distric à Maine ecrit à New Glocester, 1797,* Courtesy, Henry Francis du Pont Winterthur Museum, Joseph Downs Manuscript Collection (hereafter DMMC, WM), no. 61X69, Winterthur, Del.

6. Emery, p. 245.

7. Ibid., p. 200.

8. Indenture of Sarah Wade, DMMC, WM, 76X98.117.

9. Cotton Mather, *Elizabeth in her Holy Retirement: An Essay to Prepare a Pious Woman for her Lying In* (Boston: B. Green, 1710), pp. 6–7.

10. Dr. Alexander Hamilton, *Outlines of the Theory and Practice of Midwifery* (Northampton: Thomas Andrews & Penneman, 1797, 3rd American ed.; first pub. in 1775), p. 214.

11. Drinker diary, July 1, 1781.

12. Ibid., December 5, 1794.

13. Charles Francis Adams, *Familiar Letters of John Adams and his Wife Abigail Adams, During the Revolution with a Memoir of Mrs. Adams* (Boston: Houghton Mifflin Co., 1875), p. 95.

14. *Diary of Cotton Mather,* vol. 2, (New York: Frederick Ungar Publishing Co., 1957), p. 104.

15. [William Kenrick], *The Whole Duty of a Woman . . . By a Lady,* vol. 1, (Exeter, N. H.: Stearns & Winslow, 1794), p. 50.

16. William Buchan, *Advice to Mothers . . .* (Philadelphia: John Bioren, 1804), p. 129.

17. Journal of Esther Burr, April 13, 1756, Beinecke Rare Book and Manuscript Library, Yale University Library, New Haven.

18. John Fanning Watson, *Annals of Philadelphia . . . and New York City* (Philadelphia: E. L. Carey & A. Hart, 1830), p. 350.

19. Drinker diary, June 7, 1794.

20. Albert Cook Myers, ed., *Sally Wister's Journal, 1777–1778* (Philadelphia: Ferris & Leach, 1902), p. 182.

21. Lady Pennington, "An Unfortunate Mother's Advice to her Daughters," *The Lady's Pocket Library* (Philadelphia: Mathew Carey, 1792), p. 146

22. "Letter from a Brother to a Sister at a Boarding School," *Ladies Magazine,* November, 1792, p. 260.

23. [Eliza Ware Rotch Farrar], *The Young Lady's Friend,* By a Lady (Boston: American Stationers' Co.; John B. Russell, 1837), p. 122.

24. Ibid., p. 14.

## Chapter 2

1. Barbara Sicherman, "American History," *Signs: Journal of Women in Culture and Society* 1 (Winter, 1975): p. 467.

2. Diary of Elizabeth Drinker, January 15, 1799, Historical Society of Pennsylvania, Philadelphia.

3. Sarah Anna Emery, *Reminiscences of a Nonagenarian* (Newburyport, Mass.: William H. Huse & Co., 1879), p. 221.

4. Mrs. Sigourney, "The Schoolmistress," *The Token* (Boston: S. G. Goodrich & Co., 1830), p. 295.

5. Samuel Sewall to Edward Hull, March 28, 1687, and Samuel Sewall to David Allen, March 28, 1687, "The Letter-Book of Samuel Sewall," collection of Massachusetts Historical Society, 6 ser. 1 (1886) p. 44.

6. Alice Morse Earle, ed., *Diary of Anna Green Winslow* (Boston and New York: Houghton Mifflin Co., 1894), p. 17.

7. Inventory of Elizabeth Brunson, April 26, 1694, *Early Connecticut Probate Records,* vol. 5 (Hartford: Charles William Manwaring Co., R. S. Peck & Co., 1904), p. 414.

8. Emery, p. 21.

9. Albert Cook Myers, ed., *Sally Wister's Journal, 1777–1778* (Philadelphia: Ferris & Leach, 1902), p. 159.

10. Mrs. Caroline Gilman, *Recollections of a Housekeeper* (New York: Harper & Co., 1834), pp. 10–11.

11. Anne Holme Livingston, *Nancy Shippen: Her Journal Book . . . ,* ed. Ethel Armes (Philadelphia: J. B. Lippincott Co., 1935), p. 43.

12. Olney Winsor to his wife, February 22, 1787, Letters of Olney Winsor, 1786–1788, Virginia State Library, Richmond, Va.

13. Charles Francis Adams, *Familiar Letters of John Adams and his Wife Abigail* (Boston: Houghton Mifflin Co., 1875), pp. 240–42.

14. Elizabeth Cometti, ed. and trans., *Seeing America and Its Great Men: The Journal and Letters of Count Francesco dal Verme 1783–1784* (Charlottesville: University Press of Virginia, 1969), p. 32.

15. Account of Betsey Dorsey, folder of teacher Maria Rosina Schulze, 1750–1817, Moravian Archives, Bethlehem, Pa.

16. Emily Noyes Vanderpoel, compiler, *Chronicles of a Pioneer School from 1792 to 1833,* ed. Elizabeth C. Barney Buel (Cambridge, Mass.: University Press, 1903), p. 46.

17. Eliza Southgate Bowne, *A Girl's Life Eighty Years Ago* (New York: Charles Scribner's Sons, 1887), p. 13.

18. Manuscript diary of Mary S. Steen, October 29, 1853, Collection of George J. Fistrovich.

19. William Buchan, *Advice to Mothers . . .* (Philadelphia: John Bioren, 1804) p. 239.

20. Ibid., p. 236.

21. Hannah More, "The Essays for Young Ladies," *The Lady's Pocket Library* (Philadelphia: Mathew Carey, 1792), p. 53.

22. Benjamin Rush, "Thoughts upon Female Education . . . ," *The Universal Asylum and Columbian Magazine* (May, 1790), p. 288.

23. By a Lady, "On the Supposed Superiority of the Masculine Understanding," *The Universal Asylum and Columbian Magazine* (July, 1791), p. 10.

24. Bowne, p. 56.

25. Ibid., p. 60.

26. Ibid., p. 18.

27. Ibid., p. 31.

28. Emery, p. 21

29. Rush, pp. 291–92.

30. Catherine E. Beecher, *A Treatise on Domestic Economy* (New York: Harper & Brothers, 1848 ed.; first pub. in 1841), p. 37.

31. Abba Goold Woolson, *Woman in American Society* (Boston: Roberts Brothers, 1873), p. 53.

32. Bowne, p. 59.

33. Ibid., p. 102.

34. Ibid., p. 38.

35. Ibid., p. 22.

36. Ibid., p. 38.

37. F. Fenelon, *Instructions for the Education of a Daughter* rev. by Dr. George Hicks (London: Jonah Bowyer, 1707), pp. 208, 288.

38. John Gregory, "Gregory's Legacy to his Daughters," *The Lady's Pocket Library* (Philadelphia: Mathew Carey), pp. 107–10.

39. Bowne, p. 41.

40. [Eliza Ware Rotch Farrar], *The Young Lady's Friend, By a Lady* (Boston: American Stationers' Co.; John B. Russell, 1837), p. 293.

41. John Fanning Watson, *Annals of Philadelphia . . . and New York City* (Philadelphia: Henry F. Anners, 1846), p. 214.

42. Frances Wright, *Views of Society and Manners in America. . . .* (London: Longman, Hurst, Rees, Orne, & Brown, 1822), p. 391.

43. Ibid., p. 32.

## Chapter 3

1. Will of John Morris of Southwark, Philadelphia County Probate, 1782, no. 71, DMMC, WM, M1049

2. Emily Noyes Vanderpoel, compiler, *Chronicles of a Pioneer School from 1792 to 1833,* ed. Elizabeth C. Barney Buel (Cambridge, Mass.: University Press, 1903), p. 203.

3. Diary of Elizabeth Drinker, May 9, 1760, Historical Society of Pennsylvania, Philadelphia.

4. Sarah Anna Emery, *Reminiscences of a Nonagenarian* (Newburyport, Mass.: William H. Huse & Co., 1879), p. 34.

5. Samuel Sewall, "The Letter-Book of Samuel Sewall," collection of Massachusetts Historical Society, 6 ser. 1 (1886) p. 44.

6. Emery, p. 38.

7. Emery, p. 312.

8. [Mary Margaret Egerton] The Countess of Wilton, *The Art of Needle-Work* (London: Colburn, 1840), p. 354.

9. Inventory of John Turner, Probate Records of Sturbridge, Mass., Worcester County, DMMC, WM (Ph 470).

10. Emery, p. 15.

11. Philip Vickers Fithian, *Journal & Letters of Philip Vickers Fithian 1773–1774* (Charlottesville: Dominion Books, University Press of Virginia, 1968), p. 207.

12. Drinker diary, pincushion January, 1760; twezer case July, 1960; Bible cover before March 9, 1760, Historical Society of Pennsylvania, Philadelphia.

13. William Alexander, *The History of Women,* 2 vols. (Philadelphia: J. H. Dobelbower, 1796) vol. 2, p. 338.

14. Ibid., p. 343.

15. Arthur Calhoun, *A Social History of The American Family,* 2 vols. (New York: Barnes & Noble, Inc., 1945) vol. 2, p. 119.

16. Mrs. John King Van Rensselaer, *The Goede Vrouw of Mana-ha-ta . . .* (New York: Charles Scribner's Sons, 1898) pp. 234–36, 261–63.

17. Bill from Thomas Affleck to John Cadwalader, January 27, 1772, Cadwalader Collection, General John Cadwalader, Box

2, Historical Society of Pennsylvania, Philadelphia.

18. [Mrs. Mary Wray], *The Ladies Library,* By a Lady (London: pub. by Steele, printed for Jacob Touson, 1714), vol. 2, p. 161.

19. Hannah More, *Strictures on the Modern System of Female Education . . .* 2 vols., 6th ed. (London: T. Cadell, Jr., and W. Davies, 1799) vol. 1, p. 64.

## Chapter 4

1. Joseph Hopkinson, address to Pennsylvania Academy of Fine Arts, *The Port Folio* (December, 1810), p. 34.

2. Anne Holme Livingston, *Nancy Shippen: Her Journal Book . . . ,* ed. Ethel Armes (Philadelphia: J. B. Lippincott Co., 1935), pp. 220–21.

3. "Letters of Hannah Thomson, 1785–1788," *The Pennsylvania Magazine of History and Biography* vol. 14, no. 1, (1890), p. 35.

4. Sarah Anna Emery, *Reminiscences of a Nonagenarian,* (Newburyport, Mass.: William H. Huse & Co., 1879), p. 245.

5. "Letter of Rebecca Franks," *The Pennsylvania Magazine of History and Biography* vol. 23, no. 3 (1899), p. 304.

6. Emery, p. 246.

7. James H. Hutson, "Women in the Era of the American Revolution," *Quarterly Journal of the Library of Congress* (October, 1975), p. 297.

8. Accounts of the school, Moravian Archives, Bethlehem, Pa.

9. Diary of Elizabeth Drinker, May 4, 1778, Historical Society of Pennsylvania, Philadelphia.

10. Hopkinson, p. 34.

11. Paul S. Harris, "Gilbert Stuart and a Portrait of Mrs. Sarah Apthrop Morton," *Winterthur Portfolio I,* p. 210.

12. [Eliza Ware Rotch Farrar], *The Young Lady's Friend,* By a Lady (Boston: American

Stationers' Co.; John B. Russell, 1837), p. 97.

13. Emily Noyes Vanderpoel, compiler, *Chronicles of a Pioneer School from 1792 to 1833,* ed. Elizabeth C. Barney Buel (Cambridge, Mass.: University Press, 1903), p. 36.

14. Watson, *Annals of Philadelphia . . . and New York City* (Philadelphia: E. L. Carey & A. Hart, 1830), p. 176.

15. Hannah More, *Strictures on the Modern System of Female Education . . . ,* vol. 1 (London: T. Cadell, Jr., and W. Davies, 1799), p. 86.

16. Nitidia, "Letter to the Editor," *The Columbian Magazine or Monthly Miscellany . . . ,* vol. 1, no. 8 (1787), pp. 375–377.

17. "Washington's Household Account Book, 1793–1797," *The Pennsylvania Magazine of History and Biography* 29, no. 4, (1905), p. 173.

18. Mary Wollstonecraft, *Vindication of the Rights of Woman . . .* (Boston: Peter Edes for Thomas and Andrews, 1792), p. 112.

19. "New Publications," *Ladies Magazine* (August, 1792), p. 189.

20. Ibid., p. 190.

21. Drinker diary, March 6, 1799.

22. Ibid., April 22, 1796.

23. Matrimonial Republican, "On Matrimonial Obedience," *Ladies Magazine* (July, 1792), p. 66.

24. "Thoughts on Women," *Ladies Magazine* (August, 1792), p. 112.

25. L. C., "The Ladies of Philadelphia," *Port Folio IV* no. 6 (1810), p. 606.

26. Letter of Margaretta Akerly, March 23, 1796, Letters, c. 1796–1801, courtesy of the New York Historical Society.

27. Eliza Southgate Bowne, *A Girl's Life Eighty Years Ago* (New York: Charles Scribner's Sons, 1887), p. 25.

28. Mark Twain, *The Adventures of Huckleberry Finn* (New York: Charles L. Webster & Co., 1885), pp. 137–39.

29. Davida Tenenbaum Deutsch, "Washington Memorial Prints," *Antiques* 111 (February, 1977), pp. 324–331.

## Chapter 5

1. Manuscript diary of Hannah Rogers, August 3, 1827, DMMC, WM, 76x113.

2. Frances Trollope, *Domestic Manners of Americans,* vol. 1 (London: Whittaker, Treacher & Co., 1832), p. 103.

3. Ibid., pp. 103–104.

4. [Sarah Josepha Hale], "Advice to a Bride," By a Lady, *The Lady's Book* (May, 1832), p. 288.

5. Frances Wright, *Views of Society and Manners,* p. 393.

6. [Hale], Ibid., p. 289.

7. Ibid., p. 288.

8. David Paul Schuyler, "English and American Cottages, 1795–1855" (M.A. thesis, University of Delaware, 1976), pp. 41–45.

9. [Eliza Ware Rotch Farrar], *The Young Lady's Friend,* By a Lady (Boston: American Stationers' Co.; John B. Russell, 1837), p. 390.

10. [Mary Margaret Egerton] The Countess of Wilton, *The Art of Needle-Work,* (London: Colburn, 1840), p. 398.

11. Accounts of the school, John G. Kummer, July 6, 1839, Moravian Archives, Bethlehem, Pa.

12. [Egerton], Ibid., pp. 398–399.

13. Mark Twain, *Life on the Mississippi* (Boston: James R. Osgood & Co., 1883), p. 400.

14. Diary of Elizabeth Drinker, August 26, 1763; August 30, 1763; Historical Society of Pennsylvania, Philadelphia.

15. Inventory of Susan Ward, Dorchester, Mass. June 25, 1835, DMMC, WM 66 x 20.

# Glossary

The aim of this glossary is to help the reader make sense of the rather complex needlework terminology existing today. It attempts to note the relative importance of the different techniques and stitches along with the approximate dates of their greatest popularity. When more than one meaning is in common use for a term, preference has been given to the earliest meaning that the author could discover in original sources, for even during the eighteenth century more than one term was occasionally used to describe a stitch or a technique. From the mid-nineteenth century to the present, needlework terminology has increased enormously. This proliferation was due primarily to the needlework instructions that appeared in the many inexpensive magazines and books of the day, which brought knowledge of fancy needlework to all economic brackets. As the publications increased during the last half of the nineteenth century, each authoring needleworker seemed to feel compelled to rename stitches and techniques, thereby creating much confusion.

The accompanying drawings are intended more to clarify and identify stitches and techniques than to provide how-to-do-it instructions.

**Appliqué work; appliqué quilts:** Nineteenth-century terms for the sewing of one or more small pieces of fabric, in geometric or representational shapes, on top of a larger, background fabric to create a design or picture. Usually, one of three methods was used: (1) a design element, such as a tree or bird, was cut from a printed fabric and stitched to the background (this method acquired the name broderie perse in the late nineteenth century); (2) a paper or tin pattern was used for cutting the shape of the fabric to be added; or (3) part of the background fabric was removed in a desired shape and another fabric was added from underneath to fill the area (known then as the inlaid method; today it is usually called reverse appliqué). When the needleworker backed the completed appliquéd piece with

*Backstitch*

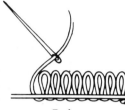

*Bed rug*

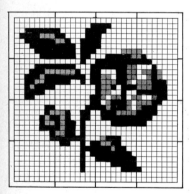

*Berlin work*

an interlining and lining and stitched the layers together, it then became an appliquéd quilt. Example of appliquéd work: Figure 122. Examples of appliquéd quilts: Plate 41; Figures 119 and 121.

**Backstitch:** The name of an embroidery stitch included in John Taylor's 1640 poem "In Praise of the Needle." This stitch creates a fine line that appears continuous. It was sometimes used for stuffed and corded work as well as for making fine scrolling lines in embroidery. Example: Figure 51.

**Bargello stitch:** Another name for Irish stitch. It did not appear in American needlework books as a substitute for the earlier term *Irish stitch* until the twentieth century.

**Bed rugs:** Called "rough woollen coverlets for beds" in Noah Webster's 1806 *Compendious Dictionary,* these were handmade rugs that are easily mistaken for hooked rugs. Running stitches with evenly raised loops of yarn were set very densely in bold patterns on wool or linen backing fabric. Made during the eighteenth or early nineteenth centuries, many originated in the Connecticut River Valley. Machine-made bed rugs were common, but few have survived. Examples: Plate 32; Figure 59.

**Berlin needlework:** See *Dresden work.*

**Berlin work:** A system of transferring printed paper patterns for needlework designs to canvas. These patterns were published in Germany in the early nineteenth century, and the finished pieces came to be called Berlin work. By the mid-nineteenth century, it was the most popular needlework form in America. Examples: Figures 107, 108, and 109.

**Berlin yarn:** Also called zephyr, German, or merino yarn and used primarily for canvas work during the nineteenth century. Spun from the fleece of merino sheep, a Spanish breed imported into the United States early in the nineteenth century, the yarn had a soft, angoralike feel. Berlin dyers were considered the world's finest, creating nearly a thousand shades for this wool. In the *Spooner & Teale Brooklyn City Directory for 1848–1849,* Mrs. Atkins said she sold "German" (yarns). Examples: Figures 107 and 109.

**Blond lace:** An eighteenth-century term for bone, bobbin, or pillow lace. Originally, blond lace meant that it was made from yarns of silk rather than cotton or linen. Advertisements mentioning blond lace (it also came in black) show it was usually imported, but Mrs. Cozani, "lately from London," advertised in *Rivington's New York Gazeteer* for July 28, 1774, that she taught "blond lace."

**Bobbin lace, bobbing, bobbinet:** Eighteenth-century names for bone, blond, or pillow lace. This technique required no needle. Instead, one stuck pins into a pillow through strategic points of a paper pattern. Then one gradually unwound thread held on bobbins or slender bones around the pins, knotting and interlocking the threads as one followed the pattern to create openwork patterns. Privately and in small shops, eighteenth-century women made money producing this lace, especially in New England around Ipswich and Boston. Miss Ingles, in the *American and Commercial Daily Advertiser* for July 10, 1827, said that besides tuition, it would cost $5.00 more to learn "working on Bobinet, in a style equal to the finest imported laces."

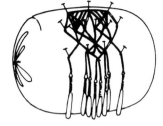

Bone lace

**Bone lace:** See *Bobbin lace.*

**Broderie perse:** A name given in the late nineteenth century to the method of appliqué work in which design elements, such as trees or butterflies, were cut from printed fabrics and sewn to a new background fabric. Usually a blind whipstitch fastened the pieces, although occasionally decorative stitches like the buttonhole, chain, or feather were used. This technique was most popular between 1780 and 1830. Examples: Figures 119 and 120.

Bullion stitch

**Bullion stitch:** An embroidery stitch resembling a little wound tube of thread. The embroiderer first took a small stitch and then wrapped the thread around the tip of the needle five to twenty turns before reinserting the needle.

**Buttonhole stitch:** An embroidery stitch with many uses and variations. When worked solidly (A), it resembles the satin stitch, with a tiny twisted edging along one side. Placed on the edge of a buttonhole slit, this edging gives strength. When worked more openly (B), the buttonhole stitch simulates prickers on a stem (Figure 57). Variations of the buttonhole stitch (C) were the major stitches used for cut work lace.

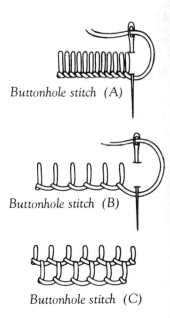

Buttonhole stitch (A)

Buttonhole stitch (B)

Buttonhole stitch (C)

**Candlewicking:** A hand-embroidered or machine-made needlework technique; both methods were popular early in the nineteenth century. In either method the principal decoration was raised stitches of soft candlewicking or roving yarns. A look at the reverse side quickly reveals any machine-made specimen; it is very neat, lacking knots, loops, and the excess yarn that are found on handmade examples. Handmade candlewick coverlets displayed a variety of stitches, including French knots, whip, cross, satin, and bullion. Sometimes the raised stitches were clipped to form tufted areas. Examples: Figures 85 and 87.

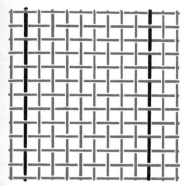

*Canvas with colored yarns*

*Chain stitch*

*Corded work*

**Canvas:** A plain-woven cloth of cotton, linen, hemp, wool, silk, etc., which often has sizing for stiffness. Canvas is used as the foundation for evenly stitched designs. The number of warp or weft threads per inch determines the size of the canvas. In the early nineteenth century, the Germans began producing canvases with a colored thread every tenth warp yarn. This helped when counting and transferring Berlin patterns (Figure 109). Penelope canvas (see page 230) was woven with warp and weft yarns in pairs. Nineteenth-century canvases tended to be much coarser than previous ones.

**Canvas work:** A term used between the seventeenth and nineteenth centuries for the art of filling the square spaces in canvas or other evenly woven background fabric with yarn to make a needleworked design. The filling yarns were crewel, silk, or metallic. Another old term sometimes used for canvas work was *tapestry work*. *Berlin work* became the term for canvas work in the nineteenth century, superseded in the twentieth century by *needlepoint*.

**Chain stitch:** A centuries-old term for an embroidery stitch worked with a needle. Its appearance resembles that of tambour work done with a hook.

**Chenille:** A fuzzy, silk yarn with a silk core. This yarn originated in France, where *chenille* means "caterpillar." It was used in American embroideries, usually only as accents, during the late eighteenth and nineteenth centuries. Sometimes the yarn was actually stitched through the background fabric with a large-eyed needle, but just as often it was couched down in rows with fine silk thread of the same shade. From the mid-nineteenth century on, a chenille yarn with a wire core was occasionally used in Berlin canvas work. Example: Figure 77.

**Corded work:** An eighteenth-century term for a technique also called Marseilles quilting. The needleworker would stitch design outlines through two layers of fabric, using fine running or backstitches. A soft cording would be stitched into the outlined channels from the back to raise design areas on the front. Frequently this technique was combined with stuffed work and flat quilting. The name *trapunto* was not applied to American corded work until the twentieth century. By 1760, machine-made examples imitating cording and stuffed work were imported into America. Example: Figure 81.

**Cotton-wool:** Another term for cotton batting. Since the eighteenth century, its primary use was as an interlining for quilts. Quilts made before the cotton gin was perfected usually reveal numerous cotton seeds in the cotton-wool when held to the light. In the *Essex Gazette* (Salem, Massachusetts) for May 11–18, 1773, Francis Grant offered "cotton-wool" for sale. Example: Figure 110.

**Crewel:** A word that at least since Shakespeare's time has meant two-ply, slackly twisted, worsted yarns and that has had a variety of spellings: crewil, cruell, cruill, crool, and crewell. Crewel yarns were well known in America and England until Berlin yarns replaced them between 1820 and 1870. Crewel yarns were revived during the late nineteenth-century Art Needlework movement and again in the mid-twentieth century. This yarn may be used for crewel embroidery, knitting, tambour, canvas work, etc. Examples of crewel embroidery: Plates 24 and 26; Figures 55, 56, 57, and 58. Examples of crewel used for canvas work: Plates 11, 13, and 14; Figures 43, 44, and 45.

*Crochet work*

**Crewel embroidery:** A modern term indicating work done with crewel yarns in a variety of stitches, not confined to a canvas or counted-thread foundation.

**Crewelwork:** A modern term indicating any needlework using two-ply, slackly twisted, worsted yarns. The work may be done on a variety of backgrounds: linen, cotton, wool, canvas, or even today's synthetics. Crewelwork was popular in America for embroidery or canvas work from the last half of the seventeenth century through the eighteenth century. It was revived in the 1870s and again in the 1950s.

*Cross-stitch (A)*

**Crochet work:** A series of chain stitches looped into each other by means of a hooked tool. It was related to tambour work, for both require a hook to create the chain stitch. In crochet work, however, the stitch is not held down to a background fabric, as in tambour work. For this reason the French, who originated crochet work, called it *crochet en l'air.* The technique spread to Ireland and was brought to the United States in the 1840s by immigrants. Instructions on crocheting appeared in *The Ladies' Work-Table Book,* published in Philadelphia in 1847. Example: the ball in Plate 34.

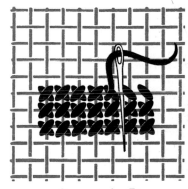

*Cross-stitch (B)*

**Cross-stitch:** A style of stitch used for centuries for embroidery and canvas work. Since it was also the predominant stitch for marking clothing, household linens, and samplers (A), it was frequently called the marking stitch (Plate 4, Figure 20). Although used in America for canvas work in the eighteenth century (Plate 15, Figure 45), cross-stitch was far more popular for Berlin work (B) in the nineteenth century. It was also called gros point in Berlin work.

**Cut work:** A method of making needle lace. An area of the background fabric was completely removed, its raw edges were secured with a holding stitch, and the empty section was filled with variations of the buttonhole stitch. Another contemporary name for this technique was pointing. Cut work seems to have been taught a few years earlier in America than was Dresden work. An early advertise-

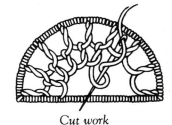

*Cut work*

*Darning sampler*

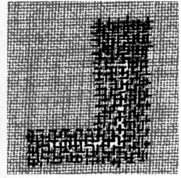

*Darning sampler*

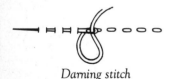

*Darning stitch*

*Dresden work*

ment was that of Martha Logan in the *South Carolina Gazette* of March 27–April 3, 1742. She taught "plain Work, Embroidery, tent and cut Work." By 1754, the same Martha Logan also advertised Dresden work. The *hollie stitch* or *hollie point* were terms used later in the nineteenth century for this work. Examples: Figures 19 and 69.

**Darning samplers:** Practice pieces designed to teach mending techniques. The needleworker tried to simulate different fabric weaves. Some samplers had deliberate tears or cuts, which were to be repaired. Darning was occasionally mentioned in advertisements, such as *Rivington's New York Gazeteer* listing for February 23, 1775, where an unidentified woman wanted a position teaching "plain Work, Darning, Marking, and Grafting." Example: Figure 27.

**Darning stitch:** Also called the running stitch, it consisted of small stitches, equally spaced.

**Drawn work:** See *Dresden work.*

**Dresden work:** A form of needle lace worked on a background material from which certain threads in the design areas had been removed. Embroidery stitches were then woven around the area or used to draw the remaining ground yarns together into lacelike designs. The resulting work could be fairly coarse, as in Pennsylvania hand towels (Figure 70), or very fine, depending on the background fabric and filling yarns. Elinor and Mary Purcell were early advertisers of the technique, offering "Dresden on Lawn and Muslin" in *The Boston Evening Post* for May 13, 1751. Also called weave lace, as in Lucy Brown and Ann Ball's January 3, 1771, announcement in the *Pennsylvania Gazette:* "Sisters, Natives of England, lately arrived from Paris," who would teach "weave lace." Mrs. Anderson in the *Pennsylvania Gazette* for April 12, 1759, used a rare term, *Berlin needlework,* "all Manner of Berlin or Dresden NEEDLEWORK." (Berlin work, the canvas-work technique of the nineteenth century, was not yet in use. It was called drawn work more and more during the nineteenth century.)

**Family register:** Another eighteenth- and nineteenth- century name for genealogical samplers. Examples: Plate 8; Figure 29.

**Fancywork:** Until at least the mid-nineteenth century, this term included all the embroidery and canvas-work stitches and techniques. Except for women who had been trained as professional embroiderers, only those with leisure time and a needlework education practiced fancywork. To do fancywork, therefore, implied that the needleworker had attained a certain level of social stature.

**Feather stitch:** One of the few embroidery stitches specifically mentioned in an American newspaper advertisement. Eleanor Druitt in the *Boston Gazette* for March 21, 1774, said she taught "Feather-Stitch" along with a long list of other popular techniques. It was probably a novelty that Mrs. Druitt advertised because American embroidery of the eighteenth century rarely contained the feather stitch.

**Fern stitch:** One of the names mentioned in John Taylor's 1640 poem "In Praise of the Needle." In American embroidery, the major use of it was to stitch the foliage of weeping willow trees in mourning pictures. Example: Figure 77.

**Flame stitch:** A twentieth-century name for the Irish stitch used for canvas work.

**Flat quilting:** A decorative, rather than utilitarian, style of quilting that used two layers of fabric and had no interlining. This allowed the needleworker to do even finer stitches than on one-piece quilts, sometimes gathering areas slightly to form puckering. Popular in England, flat quilting was most often used in America to decorate the smooth areas of stuffed and corded pieces.

**Flat stitch:** A stitch very similar to the Roumanian couching stitch—both cover areas solidly and show more thread on the front (A) than on the reverse side (B). There was less twist on the surface of the flat stitch than on the Roumanian couching because of the direction in which the needle entered the fabric at the top of each row.

**Florentine stitch:** A term that first appeared in American needlework books late in the nineteenth century to replace the earlier term *Irish stitch.*

**French knot:** An embroidery stitch that creates a tiny, circular knot. Small areas of closely set French knots formed an interesting texture and were often used on canvas work and embroidery to form flower centers or sheep's wool.

**Genealogical sampler:** A needlework piece that lists the members of a family in chart form, as in Figure 29, or more ingeniously, as fruit on a family tree, as in Plate 8. American genealogical samplers were made sporadically throughout the eighteenth century, but became particularly fashionable between 1800 and 1830.

**German canvas:** A canvas usually made of cotton. Every tenth warp yarn was colored to help when counting and transferring Berlin patterns. Example: Figure 109.

**German yarn:** See *Berlin yarn.*

*Feather stitch*

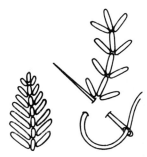

*Fern stitch*

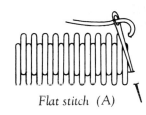

*Flat stitch (A)*

*Flat stitch (B)*

*French knot*

*Hatchment*

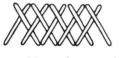

*Herringbone stitch*

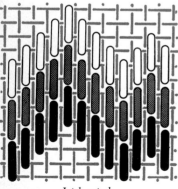

*Irish stitch*

**Hatchments:** Coats of arms—embroidered, drawn, or painted and usually of lozenge shape. In the 1806 *Compendious Dictionary,* Noah Webster called a hatchment an "escutcheon set up for the dead." By this he meant that the family would hang theirs in the church or in their house whenever a family member died. Examples: Plates 11 and 35.

**Herringbone stitch:** Known by this name as early as the eighteenth century, it is a loosely worked embroidery stitch, resembling a lattice. More recent names are ladder, shadow, long-armed cross, or mossoul cross-stitch.

**Hollie stitch** or **hollie point:** See *Cut work.*

**Hungarian** or **point d'hongrie stitch:** Names used in American needlework books only after the late nineteenth and twentieth centuries as a substitute for the earlier term *Irish stitch.* Point d'hongrie in the early eighteenth century referred to a coarse French fabric woven on a loom in a zigzag design, usually used for wall and perhaps bed hangings.

**Inlaid work:** A rare variation of appliqué quilting, practiced from the middle of the eighteenth century to early in the nineteenth century. Today it is sometimes called *reverse appliqué.* The quilter cut her design out of the background fabric, turned the edges under to prevent raveling, then laid colored fabrics under the open areas, and stitched both layers together. In the *Georgia Gazette* (Savannah) of November 2, 1774, William Obryen offered 40 shillings as reward for "A BED QUILT" stolen from his bed, which had in "the middle [a] large tree (inlaid work) with a peacock at the root and five small birds on the branches."

**Irish stitch:** Perhaps the favorite canvas-work stitch in the eighteenth century. It was a fast-moving, vertical stitch on the surface, which progressed three to four squares at one time. From the early seventeenth century until the 1880s, it was known in England and America by this name. Then it began to be called the *Florentine* and gradually, *bargello, Hungarian,* and *flame stitch.* Mrs. Wright in the *South Carolina Gazette* (Charleston) of July 13–20, 1747, said she taught the "Irish stitch." Examples: Plates 12, 14, and 16; Figures 46 and 47.

**Knitting:** An ancient method of making a stretchable fabric. Using two or more narrow, long pins as needles, the knitter looped yarn in a way so as to form an interlocked fabric. Some women knit elaborate stitches, mixed yarn colors, or even knitted lace. Examples: Plate 20; Figure 6.

**Mantua-maker:** The eighteenth- and early nineteenth-century term for a dress-maker.

**Map sampler:** Produced in limited numbers in the United States; more popular in England. The art teacher James Cox advertised in the *Pennsylvania Packet* for September 2, 1790, that he accurately copied "Copperplate Prints, Maps and Paintings" for needlework.

**Marking:** The common term for adding an identifying device, letter, or number on fabric articles. Alphabets and numbers were worked (usually in the cross-, or marking, stitch) on simple samplers as patterns to be referred to for marking clothing and household linens. Example: Figure 20.

**Marking stitch:** See *Cross-stitch.*

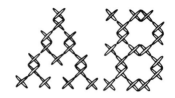

*Marking stitch*

**Marseilles quilting:** In the eighteenth century, this term included two different techniques. Advertisements show that before 1760 it was an entirely handmade product that resembled stuffed or corded work. Early advertisements called it loom quilting or mock quilting, as well as Marseilles quilting. By 1760, the machine-made product was imported to America. Both handmade and woven products remained popular until about 1830, when the machine-made product, by then woven on the Jacquard loom, dominated. Examples of handmade: Figures 81 and 83.

**Merino yarn:** See *Berlin yarn.*

**Metallic sewing:** A style of sewing that used yarns made with very thinly drawn gold, silver, or brass wire wound around a core of silk. Large-eyed needles were used to sew the metallic yarns to prevent damaging the wrapped metal. Occasionally narrow, flat, metallic yarns without a core were also used. Example: Plate 35.

**Needle-lace work:** A term used by teacher Ruth Hern in the *Boston News-Letter* for March 9, 1775. She probably meant that she taught both cut work and Dresden work, as opposed to bobbin or bone lace.

**Needlepoint:** Essentially a twentieth-century term used as a substitute for the earlier contemporary term *canvas work.* Today *needlepoint* may also occasionally indicate the popular tent stitch.

**Net:** Before the nineteenth century, the term indicated a finely meshed fabric made by a needle or pillow-lace technique. Machinery for making net was developed early in the nineteenth century. Net, either hand- or machine-made, was the foundation fabric for netted lace. Sarah Hays in the June 9, 1768, *Pennsylvania Gazette,* advertised that she taught "net work." Example: center of white embroidery: Figure 71.

**Netted lace:** A form that required a foundation of hand- or machine-made net. The needlewoman then used embroidery stitches to fill in some of the meshes to form lacelike designs.

**Netting:** An art for making fish nets, practiced in all seacoast areas. A netting needle was a long, slim rod with a slit at each end to wind the thread. After fastening the first loop to something firm, the rest of the stitches or loops were built on it by knotting the thread at regular intervals. While the knots were being formed, different-sized gauges (bone or ivory sticks) were held as the meshes were formed so that the holes would all be of a uniform size. This work was used for trimming. Example: fringe on Figure 86.

**One-piece quilts:** Those quilts in which the top layer was a single fabric (or several widths sewn together, as opposed to pieced or appliquéd tops). They were most popular during the eighteenth century. Since they had no other decoration, one-piece quilts characteristically had elaborate quilted designs worked in fine running or backstitches. Examples: Figures 111, 112, and 113.

**Outline stitch:** See *Whipstitch.*

**Patches:** Pieces of printed fabrics, often used for making appliquéd quilts. Rebecca Amory in *The Boston Evening Post* for October 10, 1763, said she had "English & India Patches" for sale. Probable examples: Figures 119 and 120.

**Patchwork:** An eighteenth- and nineteenth-century term apparently used indiscriminately to describe the pieced or appliquéd techniques. In the 1782 Baltimore County probate record of James Kingsbury is listed "1 Counterpin patch work— 45 shillings."

**Penelope canvas:** Canvas woven with paired warp and weft yarns. Developed in the mid-nineteenth century, it allowed the needlewoman to separate the paired threads and work specific areas twice as finely as other portions. Mention and a drawing of penelope canvas in a description of an antimacassar appeared in the May, 1849, issue of *Godey's Magazine and Lady's Book,* page 362.

**Petit point:** A French term, used only rarely in eighteenth-century America, that began to appear in nineteenth-century sewing books to mean the tent stitch. The tent, or petit point, stitch crossed one or two intersections of the threads of the canvas diagonally. At times, especially in the twentieth century, the term also indicates work done on today's finest-gauge canvas (12 to 24 holes to the inch).

**Pieced work** and **pieced quilts:** Nineteenth-century terms that referred to constructing a piece of fabric by stitching together smaller pieces of different fabrics. Joining

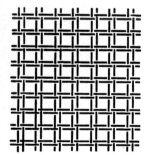

*Penelope canvas*

straight-edged pieces, and making them lie flat, was far easier than using curved ones. Only an accomplished needlewoman attempted designs like the one in Figure 117. When the needleworker added a lining and interlining and stitched through the three layers, it became a pieced quilt. Example of pieced work: Figure 117. Example of pieced quilt: Figure 116.

**Pillow lace:** See *Bobbin lace.*

**Plain sewing:** Until at least the mid-nineteenth century, this term meant stitching seams, hems, buttonholes, etc.; it usually also included knitting.

**Pointing:** See *Cut work.*

**Print work:** In needlework, the technique of using very tiny black stitches to imitate the engraved or stippled lines of a copperplate print. A favorite engraving was traced (usually by a professional) onto the silk background. A good contemporary description of a print work was given in a review of the Second Annual exhibition of the Society of Artists in the *Port Folio* of August, 1812. An entry exhibited by Mrs. Eddowes was described as "a piece of needle work in imitation of engraving in the line manner—worked on white satin with black silk, the threads of which appear like the lines of engraving." Needlework books in the 1850s were still describing this technique. Example: Figure 38.

**Queen's stitch:** The most complex of all canvas-work stitches. Each unit was made up of four or five stitches crossed in the center by a tiny horizontal stitch. Because of so many stitches entering one square, holes were formed at the top and bottom of the stitch, giving a characteristic texture to the Queen's stitch. Usually worked only in silk, this stitch was so time-consuming that it was commonly confined to small items. Elizabeth Drinker mentioned in October of 1758 that she "finish'd a Queen's stitch Pocket Book." The height of the limited vogue of the Queen's stitch seems to have been between 1780 and 1810. It has been almost totally neglected since then, although some needlework books continued to show it. Late in the nineteenth century, the name gradually changed to *rococco stitch.* Examples: Plate 20 (the pocketbooks); Figure 49.

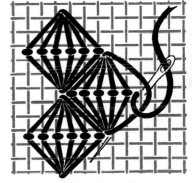

*Queen's stitch*

**Quilting:** The process of fastening three layers of fabric together, usually with running, back, or machine stitching. The top layer may have embroidery, piecing, or appliqué decoration applied before being quilted. But in the so-called one-piece quilt, the quilting stitches themselves were the only decoration. During the Victorian era, spaced ties, or tufting, substituted for stitching. Examples: appliquéd quilt, Figure 121; one-piece quilt, Figure 112; pieced quilt, Figure 116.

**Quilts:** Warm bed coverings made from three layers of fabric: a top piece most commonly of cotton, wool, linsey-woolsey, or silk; an interlining, of cotton-wool, woven wool, or eider down; and the lining, of cotton, silk, linen, linsey-woolsey, or wool. The needlewoman stitched through these three layers, creating various designs. Besides being made in the home, quilts were imported ready-made or professionally quilted. On November 25, 1776, Elizabeth Evans advertised in the *New York Gazette and Weekly Mercury* that she "wrought quilts."

**Ribbon work:** A form that used specially shaded and dyed narrow silk ribbons instead of yarn or thread to work embroidery designs. It was popular early in the nineteenth century, especially at the Moravian schools. Although seldom worked later in the nineteenth century, ribbon work was given a new name—rococco work.

**Rococco stitch:** A mid- to late-nineteenth-century name for the Queen's stitch used in canvas work.

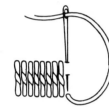

*Roumanian couching (A)*

*Roumanian couching (B)*

**Roumanian couching stitch:** An embroidery stitch used to cover areas solidly. Its surface appearance is not as smooth as the satin stitch, because of the twist made by the small stitches taken at the top and bottom of each row (A). The reverse side shows only these small stitches (B). Other modern names are Oriental, New England laid, economy, Roman, figures, and overlaid stitch. Example: Figure 55.

**Running stitch:** Small, straight stitches evenly spaced. Basic to plain sewing for seaming, darning, quilting, and gathering areas, it was also an early decorative stitch when varied slightly. One variation, used for early black work, required a second running stitch to follow the first, filling in the original spaces. Another variation was used for many bed rugs, on which a raised loop was formed by not pulling the yarn flat on the material.

**Sampler:** A needlework form recording stitches and designs, often but not necessarily signed and dated. Samplers functioned primarily as a reference work and as a statement of ability. Also called sams or examplars. American ones survive from as early as the mid-seventeenth century. Examples: Plates 3 and 6; Figures 18, 20, and 22.

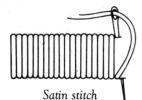

*Satin stitch*

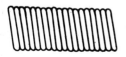

*Satin stitch (back)*

**Satin stitch:** An embroidery stitch that is useful for covering areas solidly. The stitch, worked in a compact fashion, uses as much yarn on the back as on the front. It is possible to work the satin stitch so neatly that the back appears almost identical to the front. In American crewelwork, this stitch was rarely used except to fill small accent areas.

**Satin-stitch pictures:** The name for a form of needlework popular between 1785 and 1840, executed with silk yarns, usually on silk backgrounds. Silk work was known earlier but was far less common (Plate 7). In most satin-stitch pictures, the satin stitch predominated, filling the major portions of the design. Accents of French knots, seed, or whipstitches were used. Philadelphia's Mrs. Mallon, in her May 11, 1802, advertisement in *The Aurora General Advertiser,* listed the typical subjects as "Figure Flower, and Landscape Embroidery." Miss Lambert's 1851 *Hand-Book of Needlework,* page 87, describes her method of tracing a design "for embroidering in satin-stitch." Ironically, some of the very large solid areas of these pictures only appear to be satin stitched, for when looked at from the back of the piece, they are seen as compact rows of whipstitch. Examples: Plate 39; Figures 96 and 100.

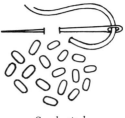

*Seed stitch*

**Seed or seeding stitch:** A term used since early in the eighteenth century to describe groups of tiny stitches that resemble random dots, often used to fill flower centers.

**Spangles:** The eighteenth-century term for sequins, made of tiny silver, gold, copper, and brass disks. An early reference to their use appeared in Mrs. Cole's advertisement in the *New York Gazette and Weekly Mercury* for April 4, 1774, saying that she would teach each person "to spangle." Spangles became most popular in the years from 1800 to 1840. Example: Figure 96.

*Spangles*

**Stuffed work:** A handmade technique for petticoats or coverlets, sometimes also called Marseilles quilting. The needleworker stitched her design outlines in fine running or backstitches. From the back she carefully eased cotton-wool through small holes to pad certain outlined areas. Frequently, this technique was combined with cording and flat quilting. Machine-made examples imitating stuffed and corded work were imported into America by 1760 and were also called Marseilles quilting. Example: Figure 83.

**Tambour work:** A needlework form that derived its name from the drum-shaped frame (Plate 10) used to stretch the fabric. Instead of a needle, a tiny hook (Figure 73) drew a loop of thread from below the fabric to the surface. Reinserting the hook and repeating this operation produced a chain stitch much faster than using a needle. The technique was probably originated in India, where a frame was not used. The French introduced the frame as well as the name. Perhaps the earliest to mention this work in America was Mrs. Bontamps, a French emigré milliner, in the *Pennsylvania Gazette* for December 29, 1768, saying, "She also

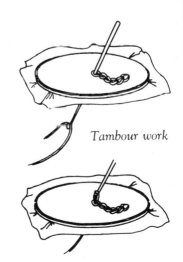

*Tambour work*

embroiders in gold, Silver, Silk and Thread, upon the late invented Tambour." The height of tambour's popularity occurred just before the end of the eighteenth century and during the early years of the nineteenth. Example: Figure 72.

**Tapestry work:** Either loom-made or handstitched canvas work. The latter often attempted to imitate the former, inspired by the output of the Gobelin factory in France. In the July 19–28, 1739, *South Carolina Gazette* (Charleston), Jane Voyer mentions several forms she taught, including "Tapistry or any other sort of Needle-work."

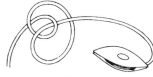

*Tatting*

**Tatting:** A process by which a pointed oval shuttle, instead of a needle, creates work similar to lace. The shuttle's thread is knotted into a series of loops around the fingers. During the eighteenth century, tatting was practiced in Europe more than in America. Example: Figure 1, the woman is tatting as she walks.

**Tent stitch:** Also spelled ten or tenth. It meant a canvas-work stitch that diagonally crossed every one or two intersections of threads of the background. The tent stitch, a popular though very old stitch, was especially useful on fine canvases for producing intricate designs and scenes. Teachers like Martha Logan in the *South Carolina Gazette* (Charleston) of August 1–8, 1754, specifically mentioned, "all kinds of Tent and Dresden Work." Before the twentieth century the stitch was worked in horizontal rows, which often pulled the background badly out of shape. Examples: Plate 13; Figures 24 and 25.

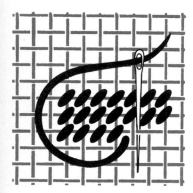

*Tent stitch*

**Trapunto:** A term applied in the twentieth century to American and English stuffed and corded work.

**Weave lace:** See *Dresden work.*

*Whipstitch*

**Whipstitch:** The name of a common embroidery stitch. The Englishman John Taylor in his 1640 poem "In Praise of the Needle" mentioned this name, which was used continuously into the nineteenth century. More modern names are the outline, stem, stalk, crewel, and rope. When the right side of the whipstitch is stretched out and worked in compact rows, it can have the appearance of a long-and-short satin stitch. Example: Figure 100.

**White work:** A term that referred to several techniques, popular in the early nineteenth century, worked on white fabrics with white yarns. Examples of white work included candlewicking, Marseilles quilting, and white embroidery. Examples: Figures 83, 84, and 85.

**Zephyr yarn:** See *Berlin yarn.*

# Suggested Readings

## On Needlework

Baker, Muriel L. *The A B C's of Canvas Embroidery.* Sturbridge: Old Sturbridge Village, 1968.

Bolton, Ethel Stanwood, and Coe, Eva Johnston. *American Samplers.* 1921. Reprint. Princeton: The Pyne Press, 1973.

Caulfield, S[ophia] F[rances] Anne, and Saward, Blanche C. *The Dictionary of Needlework: An Encyclopedia of Artistic, Plain, and Fancy Needlework.* Dealing fully with the details of all the stitches employed, the method of working, the materials used, the meaning of technical terms, and, where necessary, tracing the origin and history of the various works described. 1882. Reprint. New York: Crown Publishers, 1972.

Colby, Averil. *Quilting.* New York: Charles Scribner's Sons, 1971.

Cooper, Grace Rogers. *The Copp Family Textiles.* Smithsonian Studies in History and Technology, no. 7. Washington, D.C.: Smithsonian Institution Press, 1971.

Davidson, Mary M. *Plimoth Colony Samplers.* Marion, Mass.: The Channings, 1975.

Davis, Mildred J. *Early American Embroidery Designs.* New York: Crown Publishers, 1969.

Deutsch, Davida Tenenbaum. "Washington Memorial Prints." *Antiques* 111 (February, 1977): 324–31.

Edwards, Joan. "A Survey of English Literature of Embroidery 1840–1940." *Bulletin of the Needle and Bobbin Club* 59 (1976): 3–19.

Garrett, Elizabeth Donaghy. "American Samplers and Needlework Pictures in the DAR Museum. Part I: 1739–1806." *Antiques* 105 (February, 1974): 356–64; "Part II: 1806–1840" *Antiques* 107 (April, 1975): 688–701.

Giffen, Jane C. "Susanna Rowson and Her Academy." *Antiques* 98 (September, 1970): 436–440.

Ginsburg, Cora. "Textiles in the Connecticut Historical Society." *Antiques* 107 (April, 1975): 712–25.

Groves, Sylvia. *The History of Needlework Tools and Accessories.* London: Country Life Limited, 1966.

Grow, Judith K., and McGrail, Elizabeth. *Creating Historic Samplers.* Princeton: The Pyne Press, 1974.

Hanely, Hope. *Needlepoint in America.* New York: Charles Scribner's Sons, 1969.

Harbeson, Georgiana Brown. *American Needlework: The History of Decorative Stitchery from the Late 16th to the 20th Century.* New York: Coward-McCann, 1938.

Howe, Margery Burnham. *Early American Embroideries in Deerfield, Massachusetts.* Deerfield: Heritage Foundation, 1963.

Hughes, Therle. *English Domestic Needlework 1660–1860.* London: Abbey Fine Arts, 1961.

Landon, Mary Taylor, and Swan, Susan Burrows. *American Crewelwork.* New York: Macmillan Publishing Co., 1970.

Lane, Rose Wilder. *Woman's Day Book of American Needlework.* New York: Simon and Schuster, 1963.

Levey, Santina. *Discovering Embroidery in the Nineteenth Century.* Tring, Herts: Shire Publications, n.d.

Nylander, Jane. "Some Print Sources of New England Schoolgirl Art." *Antiques* 110 (August, 1976): 292–312.

Orlofsky, Patsy, and Orlofsky, Myron. *Quilts in America.* New York: McGraw-Hill Book Co., 1974.

Peto, Florence. *Historic Quilts.* New York: The American Historical Co., 1939.

———. "Some Early American Crewelwork." *Antiques* 59 (May, 1951): 387–90.

Ring, Betty. "The Balch School in Providence, Rhode Island." *Antiques* 107 (April, 1975): 660–71.

———. "Collecting American Samplers Today." *Antiques* 101 (June, 1972): 1012–18.

———. "Mrs. Saunders' and Miss Beach's Academy, Dorchester." *Antiques* 110 (August, 1976): 302 –311.

———, ed. *Needlework: An Historical Survey.* New York: Main Street/Universe Books, 1975.

Rowe, Ann Pollard. "Crewel Embroidered Bed Hangings in Old and New England." *Boston Museum Bulletin* 71 (1973): 101–166.

Schorsch, Anita. *Mourning Becomes America: Mourning Art in the New Nation.* [an exhibition catalog]. Clinton, New Jersey: The Main Street Press, 1976.

Sharp, Mary. *Point and Pillow Lace: A Short Account of Various Kinds, Ancient and Modern, and How to Recognize Them.* New York: E. P. Dutton & Co., 1899.

Swan, Susan Burrows. *A Winterthur Guide to American Needlework.* New York: Crown Publishers, 1976.

———. "Worked Pocketbooks." *Antiques* 107 (February, 1975): 298–303.

Taylor, Gertrude. "Mrs. Susanna Rowson, 1762–1824: An Early English-American Career-Woman." *Old-Time New England* 35 (April, 1945): 71–73.

Vanderpoel, Emily Noyes. *American Lace & Lace-Makers.* Edited by Elizabeth C. Barney Buel. New Haven: Yale University Press, 1924.

Warren, William L., ed. *Bed Ruggs: 1722–1833.* [an exhibition catalog] Hartford: Wadsworth Atheneum, 1972.

Watkins, Susan Finlay. "Connecticut Needlework in Webb-Deane-Stevens Museum." *Antiques* 109 (March, 1976): 542–44.

Wilton, The Countess of; [Mary Margaret Egerton]. *The Art of Needle-Work.* London: Colburn, 1840.

## On Women

Adams, Abigail Smith, and Adams, John. *The Book of Abigail and John: Selected Letters of the Adams Family, 1762–1784.* Edited by L[yman] H. Butterfield, Marc Friedlaender, and Mary-Jo Kline. Cambridge, Mass.: Harvard University Press, 1975.

Adams, John, and Adams, Abigail Smith. *Familiar Letters of John Adams and His Wife Abigail Adams, During the Revolution.* Edited by Charles Francis

Adams. Boston: Hurd and Houghton, 1876.

Beales, Ross W., Jr. "In Search of the Historical Child: Miniature Adult and Youth in Colonial New England." *The American Quarterly* 27 (October, 1939): 379–99.

Benson, Mary Sumner. *Women in the Eighteenth-Century America: A Study of Opinion and Social Usage.* Studies in history, economics, and public law, no. 405. Edited by the faculty of Political Science of Columbia University. New York: Columbia University Press, 1935.

Bird, Caroline. *Enterprising Women: Their Contribution to the American Economy 1776–1976.* New York: W. W. Norton & Co., 1976.

Bowne, Eliza Southgate. *A Girl's Life Eighty Years Ago: Selections from the Letters of Eliza Southgate Bowne.* Introduction by Clarence Cook. New York: Charles Scribner's Sons, 1888.

Degler, Carl N. "What Ought to Be and What Was: Women's Sexuality in the Nineteenth Century." *The American Historical Review* 79 (December, 1974): 1467–90.

DeMause, Lloyd, ed. *The History of Childhood.* New York: Harper & Row Publishers, 1975.

DePauw, Linda Grant, and Hunt, Conover. *Remember the Ladies: Women in America, 1750–1815.* [an exhibition catalog]. New York: The Viking Press, 1976.

Ditzion, Sidney. *Marriage, Morals and Sex in America: A History of Ideas.* New York: Octagon Books, 1953.

Drinker, Cecil K. *Not So Long Ago: A Chronicle of Medicine and Doctors in Colonial Philadelphia.* New York: Oxford University Press, 1937.

Drinker, Elizabeth. *Extracts from the Journal of Elizabeth Drinker, from 1759 to 1807 A.D.* Edited by Henry D. Biddle. Philadelphia: J. B. Lippincott Co., 1889.

Earle, Alice Morse. *Child Life in Colonial Days.* New York and London: Macmillan Publishing Co., 1899.

———. *Colonial Dames and Good Wives.* Boston and New York: Houghton Mifflin Co., 1895.

———. *Colonial Days in Old New York.* 5th ed. New York: Charles Scribner's Sons, 1909.

———. *Home Life in Colonial Days.* New York: Macmillan Publishing Co., 1898.

———. *Margaret Winthrop.* New York: Charles Scribner's Sons, 1895.

Emery, Sarah Anna. *Reminiscences of a Nonagenarian.* Newburyport, Mass.: William H. Huse & Co., 1879.

Fisher, Josephine. "Journal of Esther Burr." *The New England Quarterly* 3 (April, 1930): 297–315.

Frost, William Jerry. *The Quaker Family in Colonial America: A Portrait of the Society of Friends.* New York: St. Martin's Press, 1973.

Jefferson, Thomas. *The Family Letters of Thomas Jefferson.* Edited by Edwin Morris Betts and James Adam Bear, Jr. Columbia, Mo.: University of Missouri Press, 1966.

Langdon-Davies, John. *A Short History of Women.* New York: The Viking Press, 1928.

"The Life and Age of Woman." *Quarterly Journal of the Library of Congress.* Supplement to Annual Report of the Library of Congress. Sarah L. Wallace, ed. Washington, D.C.: Government Printing Office 32 (October, 1975): 1-370.

Livingston, Anne Holme. *Nancy Shippen: Her Journal.* Edited and compiled by Ethel Armes. Philadelphia: J. B. Lippincott Co., 1935.

Marlow, H. Careton, and Davis, Harrison M. *The American Search for Woman.* Santa Barbara, Calif.: Clio Books, 1976.

Melder, Keith. "Mask of Oppression: The Female Seminary Movement in the United States." *New York History* 55 (July, 1974): 261–79.

Morgan, Edmund S., ed. *The Puritan Family: Religion and Domestic Relations in Seventeenth-Century New England.* 2d rev. ed. New York: Harper & Row Publishers, 1967.

———. *Virginians at Home: Family Life in the Eighteenth Century.* Williamsburg: Colonial Williamsburg, 1952.

Morris, Richard B. *Studies in the History of American Law: With Special Reference to the Seventeenth and Eighteenth Centuries.* 2d ed. Philadelphia: Joseph M. Mitchell Co., 1959.

Orenstein, Gloria Feman. "Art History." *Signs: Journal of Women in Culture and Society* 1 (Winter, 1975): 505–25.

Rothman, David J., and Rothman, Sheila M., eds. *The Colonial American Family: Collected Essays.* New York: Arno Press & *The New York Times*, 1972.

Rudolph, Frederick, ed. *Essays on Education in the Early Republic: Benjamin Rush, Noah Webster, Robert Coram, Simeon Doggett, Samuel Harrison Smith, Amable-Louis-Rose de Lafitte du Courteil, Samuel Knox.* Cambridge: Harvard University Press, Belknap Press, 1965.

Ryan, Mary P. *Womanhood in America: From Colonial Times to the Present.* New York: New Viewpoints, Division of Franklin Watts, 1975.

Scott, Anne Frior. *The Southern Lady: From Pedestal to Politics, 1830–1930.* Chicago: University of Chicago Press, 1970.

Sicherman, Barbara. "American History." *Signs: Journal of Women in Culture and Society* 1 (Winter, 1975): 461–86.

Spruill, Julia Cherry. *Women's Life and Work in the Southern Colonies.* New York: Russell & Russell, 1969.

Thompson, Roger. *Women in Stuart England and America: A Comparative Study.* London and Boston: Routledge & Kegan Paul, 1974.

Trumbull, Harriet, and Trumbull, Maria. *A Season in New York in 1801: Letters of Harriet and Maria Trumbull.* Edited by Helen Morgan. Pittsburgh: University of Pittsburgh Press, 1969.

Vanderpoel, Emily Noyes, compiler. *Chronicles of a Pioneer School From 1792 to 1833, Being the History of Miss Sarah Pierce and her Litchfield School.* Edited by Elizabeth C. Barney Buel. Cambridge: The University Press, 1903.

Van Rensselaer, [May], Mrs. John King. *The Goede Vrouw of Mana-Ha-Ta: At Home and in Society, 1609–1760.* New York: Charles Scribner's Sons, 1898.

Wallace, Sarah L., ed. "The Life and Age of Woman." *Quarterly Journal of the Library of Congress* 32 (October, 1975): 1–370. Supplement to Annual Report of the Library of Congress. Washington, D.C.: Government Printing Office.

Welter, Barbara. "The Cult of True Womanhood: 1820–1860." *American Quarterly* 18 (Summer, 1966): 151–74.

Winslow, Anna Green. *Diary of Anna Green Winslow, a Boston Schoolgirl of 1771.* Edited by Alice Morse Earle. Boston and New York: Houghton Mifflin Co., 1894.

Wister, Sally. *Sally Wister's Journal: A True Narrative Being a Quaker Maiden's Account of Her Experiences with Officers of the Continental Army, 1777–1778.* Edited by Albert Cook Myers. Philadelphia: Ferris & Leach, 1902.

Wood, Clive, and Suitters, Beryl. *The Fight for Acceptance: A History of Contraception.* Aylesbury: Medical and Technical Publishing Co., 1970.

Woody, Thomas. *A History of Women's Education in the United States.* 2 vols. New York: Science Press, 1929.

Woolson, Abba Gould. *Woman in American Society.* Boston: Roberts Brothers, 1873.

## Rare Books

Alexander, William. *The History of Women, from the Earliest Antiquity, to the Present Time: Giving an Account of Almost Every Interesting Particular Concerning That Sex, Among All Nations, Ancient and Modern.* 2 vols. Philadelphia: J. H. Dobelbower, 1796. Also published in England, 1779 and France, 1791–94; title varies slightly.

Buchan, William. *Advice to Mothers, on the Subject of Their Own Health; and on the Means of Promoting the Health, Strength, and Beauty of Their Offspring.* Philadelphia: John Bioren, 1804. Published in various editions in England and America during the first decades of the nineteenth century.

———. *Domestic Medicine; or, The Family Physician: Being an Attempt to Render the Medical Art More Generally Useful, by Showing People What Is in Their Own Power Both with Respect to the Prevention and Cure of Diseases. Chiefly Calculated to Recommend a Proper Attention to Regimen and Simple Medicines.* 3d American ed. Boston: Printed by John Trumbull for Robert Hodge, J. D. M'Dougall and William Green, 1778. At least 22 editions appeared between 1771 and 1840, and by 1795 the book had

been revised and adapted to the diseases and climate of the United States; title varies slightly.

[Farrar, Eliza Ware (Rotch)]. *The Young Lady's Friend, by a Lady.* Boston: American Stationers' Co.: John B. Russell, 1836. Published anonymously at first, the book was reprinted at least twice in the next five years. In the 1870s and 1880s, shortly after the author's death, it was again republished with revisions.

Hitchcock, Enos. *Memoirs of the Bloomsgrave Family. In a series of letters . . . Containing Sentiments on a Mode of Domestic Education, Suited to the Present State of Society, Government, and Manners, in the United States of America: and on the Dignity and Importance of the Female Character.* 2 vols. Boston: Thomas and Andrews, 1790. One of several books on proper decorum written by the Rev. Hitchcock between 1785 and 1800.

Hosmer, William. *The Young Lady's Book; or, Principles of Female Education.* Auburn, N.Y.: Derby and Miller, 1851. Hosmer was also concerned with the proper education of young men and the issue of slavery.

[Kenrick, William]. *The Whole Duty of a Woman . . . By a Lady. Written at the Desire of a Noble Lord.* Exeter, N.H.: Printed and sold by Stearns & Winslow, 1794. The first edition appeared in London, 1753 and during the next seventy years was reprinted in America, intact and with revisions.

More, Hannah. *Strictures on the Modern System of Female Education With a View of the Principles and Conduct Prevalent Among Women of Rank and Fortune.* 2 vols., 6th ed. London: T. Cadell, Jun., and W. Davies, 1799. Printed at various dates in England and America during the late eighteenth and early nineteenth centuries. By 1806, ten editions had been published. More was a prolific writer, particularly on the subject of Christian behavior and domestic morality.

Peale, Charles Willson. *An Essay to Promote Domestic Happiness.* Philadelphia: Kimber & Conrad, J. Johnson, J. P. Park, T. Dobson, 1812.

Rush, Benjamin. "Thoughts upon Female Education: Accommodated to the Present State of Society, Manners, and Government of the United States of America." *The Universal Asylum* and *Columbia Magazine* (April, 1790): 209–13; (May, 1790): 288–92. Originally given as an address "to the visitors of the Young ladies' academy in Philadelphia, 28 July, 1787 at the close of the quarterly examination." Rush's remarks were then published in Philadelphia by Prichard and Hall. Within three years they were reissued by *Columbian Magazine*, whose readership was more widespread.

Watson, John Fanning. *Annals of Philadelphia being a Collection of Memoirs, Anecdotes, & Incidents of the City and its inhabitants from the Days of the Pilgrim Founders . . . To which is added an Appendix, containing Olden Time Researchers and Reminiscences of New York City.* Reprinted and revised at varying times between 1830 and 1898, portions of this also were expanded and reprinted separately.

Webster, Thomas, and Parkes, Mrs. William. *Encyclopedia of Domestic Economy: Comprising Subjects connected with the Interests of Every Individual; such as the construction of Domestic Edifices; Furniture; Carriages, and Instruments of Domestic use. Also, Animal and Vegetable substances used as Food, and the methods of Preserving and Preparing Them by Cooking; Receipts, Etc.; Materials Employed in Dress and the Toilet; Business of the Laundry; Preservation of Health, Domestic Medicines, Ec., Ec.* Edited by David Meredith Reese. New York: Harper & Brothers, 1849. Although published earlier in London, this work became most popular in America during the late 1840s and the 1850s.

Wollstonecraft, Mary. *Vindication of the Rights of Woman: With Strictures on Moral and Political Subjects.* Boston: Peter Edes for Thomas and Andrews, 1792. Published in London, Boston, and Philadelphia in the same year, this controversial book proved quite popular and was reprinted many times during the next century.

# Index